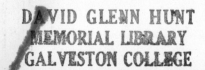

Talk of Texas

Talk of Texas

By
Jack Maguire

Illustrations by
Bob Grigsby

Shoal Creek Publishers, Inc
Austin, Texas

Library of Congress Catalog Card No. 73-84554
ISBN 0-88319-014-1

Phototypography by Photocomp, Inc., Austin, Texas

Lithographed and bound in the United States
of America by Steck-Warlick. Austin, Texas

DEDICATION

For my wife, Pat, and my sons,
Jack and Kevin - - -
Texans all.

AUTHOR'S NOTE

The stories you are about to read in this book are true. Not a single name, date or place has been changed to protect the innocent.

They have been gathered over more than 30 years of writing about Texas and Texans. They have appeared, usually in a much longer version, in such diverse publications as *The New York Times Sunday Magazine* and *True Police Cases*.

Most are from my column, "This Is Texas," which began as a regular monthly feature in *Texas Parade Magazine* in 1962 and has been published without interruption since. In 1963, the column became a weekly feature in newspapers from the Red River to the Rio Grande and from the Panhandle to the Gulf under the name "Talk of Texas."

Academicians likely would call this book a collection of Texas trivia. I like to think of it as the stuff from which real history is made — the odd, the unique, the bizarre and the humorous true stories about the people and places of a great state.

George Sessions Perry called Texas "a world in itself." In this collection of authentic stories that one doesn't usually find in the history books, I hope that Texans — and those unfortunate enough to call some less satisfying place home — will laugh a lot and learn a little as they discover Texas as it really was, and is.

Jack Maguire
Austin, Texas
June, 1973

INTRODUCTION

The story of Texas has been told and re-told, but never quite like this.

Jack Maguire is a journalist, not a historian. More than 30 years ago, he gave himself a single objective: To examine the historical and contemporary record of the sovereign and Lone Star State of Texas, and to search out the unusual and the unique.

What he has found (and which he has reported to a quarter of a million Texans each week in his syndicated newspaper column) is a delightful picture of people, places and events that one rarely finds in the history books. His stories aren't fiction, but fact. Yet if every story can't be substantiated in the nearest text that purports to record the history of Texas, the reader should not be disappointed. One must remember, with Henry Ward Beecher, that "Not that which men do worthily, but which they do successfully, is what history makes haste to record."

Jack Maguire looks beyond the successes of the worthy to find the little known, rarely-told true stories of Texas that the historians can't — or won't — put in their textbooks. And it's a kind of history that every reader, Texan or non-Texan, will find highly readable.

A native Texan, Maguire began his literary efforts at the tender age of 16. In the latter days of the Great Depression, this teen-age son of a railroad man in Denison, Texas, teamed up with a local printer to publish an eight-page monthly "lonely hearts" magazine called *The Golden Circle*. The magazine was free, but, for a dollar, an interested lonely heart could receive a picture and full description, plus name and address, of an equally lonely soul of opposite gender. Dollars in those days were as big and as hard to get your hands on as a full Texas moon, but the publishers prospered.

How Jack Maguire happened to abandon this lucrative commercialization of romance for more mundane occupations is one story he hasn't written yet. But he did try operating a steam boiler in a cleaning plant and selling Bibles door-to-door before turning to his lasting vocation of writing. Three unlikely and disparate public figures nudged him in the direction of journalism. They were W. Lee (Pappy) O'Daniel, and Franklin D. and Eleanor Roosevelt.

Long before he swooped onto the political scene with tornadic windiness and force, W. Lee O'Daniel was a Texas celebrity. He and his "Light Crust Doughboys" polluted the airwaves daily in all directions with country music and corn pone philosophizings beamed from Fort Worth. Letters from listeners and home-grown homilies in prose and poetry were grist for "Pappy" O'Daniel's radio mill. And young Jack Maguire of Denison was a regular and oft-quoted contributor.

Hearing his writings broadcast to Texas almost daily fired his zeal to write for pay, and he applied for a job on the Denison paper. The editor turned him down. Then Jack offered to bet the editor that he could produce a news story that the paper would gladly run on the front page. If he couldn't, he'd quit pestering the man for a job. If he could, he'd be made a reporter.

This was early in 1936 and Dallas was preparing to host the State's celebration of its Centennial. The enterprising young high school junior learned that President Franklin D. Roosevelt was coming to Dallas in June to open the Centennial. Through his father's railroad connections, he learned that the President's Special would come through Denison.

On a hunch, he wrote Mr. Roosevelt telling him of his bet with the editor and how badly he wanted the job as a reporter. If the President would just agree to stop off in Denison and make a speech, the youngster would have his front page story and his job. F. D. R. apparently had his own share of sporting blood; he did agree to make the speech. Jack got his first job as a reporter, and he's been writing ever since.

He has been a reporter and editor on the Denison *Herald*, Denton *Record-Chronicle* and the state capitol staff of the Associated Press. He has the unique distinction of having been editor-in-chief of two university newspapers during his student days — the *Chat* at North Texas State University and *The Daily Texan* at The University of Texas. His weekly column, "Talk of Texas," is published in more than a score of the state's newspapers.

All fledgling newspapermen yearn to fatten their pocket-books by writing magazine articles on the side, and young Maguire was no exception. His break came a year after his spectacular entry into journalism. Mrs. Eleanor Roosevelt was on one of her perennial lecture tours of the college circuit in 1937 and spoke at Southeastern State College in Durant, Oklahoma, just over the line from Denison. Because of his having brought F. D. R. to Denison, Maguire was invited to cover the lecture and meet the distinguished guest. Mrs. Roosevelt, who also wrote magazine articles, suggested to Jack that he should write a piece about how he had persuaded her husband to make a speech in a small Texas railroad town.

Thus encouraged, Maguire wrote his first magazine article and sold it, surprisingly, to *True Romances*. That confession journal ran a regular feature, "The Happiest Moment of My Life," and his experience with the President fit the pattern. Since then, the lively offspring of his prolific typewriter have appeared in such publications as *American Mercury, Railroad Magazine, The*

Rotarian, The Kiwanis Magazine, Coronet, Buick Magazine, Ford Times, the *Baltimore Sunday Sun Magazine,* the *New York Times Magazine* and many others. His monthly column, "This is Texas," has been a regular feature of *Texas Parade Magazine* since 1962.

Maguire also has edited a couple of railroad magazines of national scope, has long been a successful public relations consultant, has directed or participated in a number of successful business enterprises, has traveled throughout the world and has served, since 1956, as the Executive Director of the Ex-Students' Association of The University of Texas at Austin.

But, no matter how far afield he may range, professionally or geographically, he always comes back to Texas, and to writing about Texas.

A voracious reader and prolific writer, he has hit his full stride as a gleaner and capsuler of interesting Texas stories.

The busy world we now live in creates an exceptional demand for his particular talent. He can spot a good story anywhere and can tell it interestingly, entertainingly and informatively in amazingly few words. He knows, as J. Frank Dobie once put it, that "the most important thing is to know what to leave out of a story — not what to put into it."

You can pick up one of his columns, or one of his several books, read for a few minutes, or a few hours, and put it down without the frustration of a half-told tale. His writing is as comforting a bedside companion as an old-fashioned family doctor.

This book is a vintage distillation of many of his columns, a carefully selected and loosely organized compendium of Texana, in all its glorious variety and glamour. Jack Maguire is even more enamoured of Texas than most of the rest of us. He spins his factual yarns with the wide-eyed enchantment of Pogo, viewing "this ever-loving blue-eyed world" and marvelling at "the wonder of the wonder of it all."

Despite this approach, he is neither naive nor simply a compiler of the curious. His collections of well-told anecdotes are like mosaics, each small piece a bright spot of color in an overall pattern which is the story of Texas.

R. Henderson Shuffler
Director, Institute of Texan Cultures
San Antonio
May, 1973

STORIES THAT
HISTORY FORGOT

HOW TEXAS FORGOT— The Alamo was both a wholesale grocery and a liquor store during the 69 years it took the Legislature to recognize it as a shrine.

After the Alamo fell on March 6, 1836, ownership of the chapel and convent was in litigation. In 1847, when a quartermaster post was established there, the Army finally recognized that it was a tenant on Catholic Church property. Soldiers continued to occupy the Alamo, however, until 1879.

In that year, the Catholic Church sold the property to a merchant who converted it into a wholesale grocery. When he died, it became a wholesale liquor dispensary. Finally, in 1905, it was purchased by Clara Driscoll and the Daughters of the Republic of Texas to ensure its becoming a shrine.

FOR CONSPICUOUS BRAVERY — The only battle in history in which every participant received the Congressional Medal of Honor took place in Texas in 1874.

Col. Nelson A. Miles, moving his troops into the Panhandle following the Battle of Adobe Walls, sent out a scouting party of two civilians, a sergeant and three privates. In Hemphill County, 22 miles south of the present town of Canadian, the six were attacked by a war party of more than 100 Kiowa and Comanche Indians.

All six were wounded in the first volley fired by the Indians, but managed to get into a buffalo wallow close by. The depression was only 25 feet long and about 10 feet across, but it was deep enough to offer some protection. From that natural fortress, they held off the Indians from early morning, when the attack began, until dark.

One, an Army private named Smith, died that night. The other five, however, survived the Battle of Buffalo Wallow and recovered. All six were voted the Congressional Medal of Honor.

GENERAL HEADQUARTERS — Old Fort Clark at Brackettville probably was "home" to more famous Army brass than any other Texas post.

Between 1852, when it was founded, and 1946, when it was deactivated and converted into a guest ranch, the fort's officer roster read like an Army "Who's Who." General U. S. Grant was stationed there before the Civil War, General Phil Sheridan soldiered there and General Patton was the post commander in 1938.

Fort Clark was the last command that General Jonathan Wainwright had before he was sent to the Philippines and a place in history in World War II.

THE GAUNTLET OF SAN JACINTO — A slender white evening glove was a rallying point for the Texas Army of Independence when it routed General Santa Anna's Mexican forces at San Jacinto on April 21, 1836.

The glove was given to Captain Sidney Sherman at the farewell ball which Newport, Kentucky, citizens gave his Buckeye Volunteers as they left for Texas. A beautiful young girl tossed it to Sherman with the injunction: "Here, sir, is a gauge of battle; let it be borne foremost in the fight!"

And so the slender little glove, waving defiantly over the Texas Army's battle flag, went proudly into the attack at San Jacinto. The glove was lost in the skirmish, but the flag survived. It is displayed today behind the Speaker's rostrum in the House of Representatives at Austin.

MYSTERY MAN — Texas wanted to honor the memory of its first vice-president, Lorenzo de Zavala, by moving his body to a new resting place at San Jacinto Battleground State Park. But nobody could find his bones.

Only the stones that marked the graves in the De Zavala family cemetery have been moved. The bodies apparently have been dissolved or submerged in the muck of the Houston Ship Channel. The De Zavala burial plot has fronted the waterway for 134 years.

Lorenzo de Zavala was born in Mexico and presided at the convention that wrote the Mexican Constitution of 1824. He held many high offices in Mexico and was Santa Anna's ambassador to France when he learned that his long-time friend planned to overthrow the constitution and set himself up as dictator.

De Zavala wrote Santa Anna an angry letter of resignation, then sped to Texas to join the revolutionary movement against Mexico. He became a leader, was a signer of the Declaration of Independence and one of the drafters of the Texas Constitution. The new republic elected him its first vice-president.

When De Zavala died on November 15, 1836, he was buried in the family cemetery at the confluence of Buffalo Bayou and the San Jacinto River just across from the battleground where Santa Anna had surrendered the Mexican Army to the victorious Texans. It was from that site that Texas planned to move the graves of the De Zavala family, but no trace of the bodies was found.

WRONG HOLIDAY — Texans celebrate March 2 as their Independence Day, but the declaration actually wasn't signed until March 3.

A Texas blue norther, accompanied by rain and hail, had chilled the crude 25 by 50-foot frame building at Washington-on-the-Brazos to 38 degrees when George C. Childress called the delegates to order at 9 a.m. on March 1, 1836. They elected Richard Ellis of Peach Point as president of the convention and appointed Childress head of the committee to draw up a Declaration of Independence from Mexico.

The next day, March 2, Childress read the Declaration — a document which most historians believe that he had written long before arriving at the convention. It severed Texas' ties with Mexico and proclaimed an independent Republic. It was adopted unanimously.

However, errors were found in the copies drawn up for signing and the meeting was recessed so they could be corrected. As a result, the Declaration of Independence actually was not signed until March 3.

OUTDOOR THEATER — The first drama ever presented before a Texas audience was not staged in a theater but along the banks of the Rio Grande. The date was May 4, 1598!

Don Juan de Onate, lured by stories of a land filled with gold, was granted permission by King Philip II of Spain to conquer and settle the territory then known as New Mexico. With a troop of cavalry and a supply train of 83 wagons, De Onate began his march in Mexico City and headed north.

Early in April, 1598, the party reached the sand dunes, south of what now is El Paso, and split up. Later they were reunited after crossing the Rio Grande and De Onate decided to take formal possession of the provinces on the Rio del Norte by ordering several days of celebrations.

One of his captains, Don Miguel Farfan de los Godos, apparently was a frustrated playwright. At any rate, he turned out a comedy on the spot and staged it to the delight of the soldiers. It was the first drama ever presented on Texas soil.

DOCTOR DE VACA — Texas' first physician was Cabeza de Vaca. He also was probably the first white person to perform a surgical operation anywhere on the North American continent.

He landed on Galveston Island with 80 other Spaniards on November 6, 1528. Friendly Indians, believing that the white men had magical powers, taught De Vaca the rudiments of the crude medicine they practiced. From them he learned how to make an incision, cauterize a wound, and prepare medicine from herbs.

The first surgical operation probably was performed near where the town of Pecos now stands. The patient was an Indian who had carried an arrowhead in his right shoulder for several years. It was in 1535 that De Vaca opened the patient's chest cavity with a knife, removed the arrowhead and stitched the wound with a deer bone. The Indian recovered.

LEGENDS THAT LIVE — Did John Wilkes Booth, assassin of President Lincoln, escape punishment and live out his life in Texas?

In the late 1860's, one John St. Helen (who strongly resembled photos of Booth), turned up in Granbury, Hood County, and worked as a saloon-keeper. A sudden illness hit St. Helen one day and, thinking himself dying, he asked the saloon owner, F. J. Gordon, to send for a priest. St. Helen told them that he really was John Wilkes Booth and directed Gordon to a Granbury house where he claimed to have hidden the gun with which he shot Lincoln.

Gordon found the gun and offered it to U.S. authorities, but was told that the case was closed. Meanwhile, St. Helen recovered and moved from Granbury to Glen Rose, in Somervell County.

There he continued to tend bar. A heavy drinker himself, he delighted in reciting long passages from Shakespeare when he imbibed too heavily. Booth, of course, was a Shakespearean actor.

During his career, Booth had suffered a slight forehead wound in a bit of sword play on stage and had crushed his thumb while moving stage sets. In escaping from Ford's Theater after the assassination, he had fractured a shin bone.

When St. Helen died in 1903, his body was given a careful examination by physicians. The body revealed a nicked eyebrow, a crushed thumb bone and a shin fracture!

THE CRASH AT CRUSH — More than 30,000 people paid for the privilege of watching the most famous train wreck in the history of Texas.

The head-on collision between two trains traveling at full speed was staged September 15, 1896, as a promotion stunt by William G. Crush, general passenger agent for the Katy Railroad. For the crash site, he picked a five-mile-long piece of straight track between Waco and West in McLennan County.

The Katy then began publicizing the planned wreck all over the U.S. So many responded that dozens of special trains were operated to the site that had been renamed Crush in honor of the man who was staging the wreck. A grandstand seating 2,000 people was built.

At high noon, the crews backed their trains a mile from the collision point, tied open the locomotive throttles and leaped off. The trains were traveling an estimated 50 miles an hour when they hit head-on.

Both locomotive boilers exploded and hunks of steel hit the crowd like shrapnel. At least one man was killed, dozens were seriously injured and 30,000 were frightened within an inch of their lives.

The crash at Crush was the first and last train wreck ever staged deliberately in Texas.

MUSIC MAN — A young opera singer from Texas changed his name and his style and became the first of the nation's famous country-western music stars.

Born in Jefferson in 1883 as Marion G. Slaughter, he began recording light opera for Edison and Columbia records in 1916. However, country music (or "hillbilly," as it was called then) was beginning to catch the public's fancy and Slaughter decided to see if his operatic voice could adapt itself to these new folk songs.

Calling himself "Vernon Dalhart" — a pseudonym made up of the names of two West Texas towns — he developed a rural accent and recorded his first two numbers, "The Prisoner's Song" and "The Wreck of the Old 97". The record sold 25 million copies!

Dalhart later used as many as 50 different names in turning out hundreds of country music records that sold by the millions. He never made much money, however, because he failed to copyright his work or sign binding legal contracts. He was broke and working as a hotel night clerk when he died.

TO YOUR GOOD HEALTH — When Beaumont was an oil boom town at the turn of the century, its water supply was so bad that doctors urged the influx of new residents to drink whiskey instead.

This concerned some of the young ladies of the community who had organized an active Temperance Society years before. Hoping to save the oil field workers from the evils of alcohol, the girls boiled the local water to insure its purity. Then they dispensed it (without ice) at a dime a glass.

WELCOME TO THE U.S. — When Texas joined the Union in 1845, Massachusetts dissented. In fact, its anti-slavery legislature condemned the Republic of Texas as a foreign nation not worthy of statehood.

There the matter stood until December, 1953, when Keith Elliott, a reporter for the San Antonio *Light*, discovered Massachusetts' oversight and wrote an acid article about it. The story was picked up by the wire services and other Texas newspapers joined in a verbal barrage at the Bay State. The Yankees capitulated.

On December 29, 1953, Governor Herter formally advised Governor Allan Shivers of Texas that the Massachusetts Legislature had finally recognized the Lone Star State as a member of the Union.

HOW IT BEGAN — Texas' first television program lasted exactly 49 minutes. The star was the President of the United States.

WBAP-TV, Fort Worth-Dallas, was the first commercial television station in the Southwest and the 35th in the U.S. It went on the air at 1:58 p.m. September 27, 1948, from the Texas & Pacific Railway Station in Fort Worth where a special train carrying President Harry Truman was due to arrive 17 minutes later.

The train did pull in at 2:18 p.m. and the station pointed its three cameras at Mr. Truman and his party. The viewing audience was estimated at only 2,000 — far fewer than saw Mr. Truman in person — because there were only 400 television sets then in the entire Dallas-Fort Worth metropolitan area.

TEXANISCHE LIEDER — Some of the first songs ever written about Texas were composed by the man whose "Deutschland Uber Alles" was to become the national anthem of Germany.

He was Hoffman von Fallersleben, who had hoped to emigrate to Texas himself. When his plan to come to the New World failed, he consoled himself by writing some 30 songs about Texas. He had them published and sent to Adolph Fuchs, a Lutheran minister who had brought a German colony to Texas in 1845.

Today a copy of that song book, *Texanische Lieder*, is worth a small fortune to collectors. Only one such copy is known to exist.

CUSTER'S TEXAS STAND — Ten years before General George Custer won a kind of immortality for his tragic "last stand" against the Indians at Little Big Horn, he was the military dictator of Texas.

Custer, only 25 but already a brevet major-general, arrived in Austin shortly before Christmas, 1865, to take command of the Army of Occupation that was an aftermath of the defeat of the Confederacy. His headquarters, changed but little after more than a century, are still used by The University of Texas and form a part of what is known as the "Little Campus."

Actually, Custer was well liked by Texans and Mrs. Custer later described their tour of duty in Austin as among the happiest periods of their lives.

SAFETY FIRST — One of the most famous safety slogans of all time is credited to the agile mind of a Texas railroad ticket agent.

In the mid-1930's, J. E. Johnston, agent at the Katy station in Denison, began writing safety messages and tacking them onto the depot bulletin board. One which is still seen along highways everywhere read:

"If you drive, don't drink;
If you drink, don't drive."

CUE TO FRUSTRATION, MAYBE? — Texas will be remembered, especially around pool halls, as the birthplace of the circular pocket billiards table.

Dr. Robert D. Perry, a mathematics professor at Texas A. & I. College in Kingsville, designed and built the first round pool table in 1957, and specialists with the cue and the eight-ball haven't been the same since. Even lifetime practitioners of the game, as it is played on the orthodox rectangular table, find that their best techniques fail them when they try Perry's invention.

This doesn't bother the professor, because the game is catching on. The manufacturer to whom he sold the marketing rights sells about 40 of the round pool tables each year — at from $500 to $1,000 each.

THE LAST WORD — Briton Bailey was a Texan who never looked up to any man.

He settled in the Brazos River bottoms even before Stephen F. Austin brought his colony to Texas, and was among those Austin sought to evict as being an undesirable character. Later,

Bailey and Austin made their peace, and Brit became a captain of Texas militia. He built the first brick residence in Austin's colony, and the land he owned in Brazoria County is still known to old-timers as Bailey's Prairie.

In 1883, Bailey fell sick. His death-bed wish was to be buried standing up "with my face to the setting sun" so that the world will say, "There stands Brit Bailey."

Even in death, Brit Bailey didn't want to bow his head to any man.

DEAD-EYE AD — Although many have tried, no man in history has ever equaled the marksmanship of a quiet Texan named Ad Toepperwein.

During a ten-day marathon rifle-shooting exhibition at San Antonio in 1907, he fired 72,500 times at 2-1/4 inch wood blocks tossed into the air by aides. He missed only nine!

Born in Boerne, Kendall County, in 1869, Toepperwein was shooting ducks on the wing with a .22 rifle by the time he was five. By the time he was 20, he was appearing on vaudeville stages as the original "Dead-Eye Dick." He died in 1962.

POST WAS TOASTED — Shortly after the late cereal king, C. W. Post, bought 300 square miles of Garza County pasture in 1906 and decided to convert it into small cotton farms, a searing drought threatened the crops. The small farmers feared certain bankruptcy, but Post decided to fight.

At 15 strategic spots around his new town of Post, he stored caches of dynamite. Each time the humidity got as high as 75 percent and the wind died down, Post would fire off the explosives at each of his "battle stations."

He theorized that the blasts would force the humid air to higher altitudes where it would condense and produce rainfall. His theory proved to be practical, and on seven of the 13 occasions when he tried his novel idea, the rains came and the cotton crop was saved.

LONE STAR BIRD MAN — John James Audubon, the man who made bird-watching one of the national pastimes, might have been a Texan — but wasn't.

Born in Santo Domingo in 1785, he moved to Kentucky in 1807. In 1837, he cruised the Gulf of Mexico studying coastal wildlife. He reached Galveston on April 24, spent three weeks studying the birds on the island, then went to Houston. There he met President Sam Houston and his cabinet and captivated them.

So taken with Audubon were the officials of the Republic of Texas that they introduced a bill in the Senate on May 25, 1837, to make the naturalist a citizen. The bill was never reported out of Committee, however, and Audubon died in New York in 1851 without ever becoming a Texan.

SOPHISTICATED PIONEERS — Texas' early frontiersmen were hardly the uncouth, gun-toting ruffians so dear to the hearts of television script writers. The majority were well educated sophisticates and most were linguists of no mean ability.

One such was Louis von Hagen, former Prussian army captain, who, at the 25th anniversary of the founding of Fredericksburg, called the square dances at the Bismarck Garten — in French! And at Sisterdale, in nearby Kendall County, settlers in the 1840's conducted the meetings of their scientific and philosophical society in Latin.

FIDDLING JUSTICE — When Judge R. E. B. Baylor rode the Texas judicial circuit more than a century ago, he dispensed music and religion along with justice.

An ordained Baptist minister, he always carried a Bible, a law book and a fiddle in his buckboard. He liked to announce his arrival in town with a rousing concert, followed by a fiery sermon. Once these preliminaries were over, he was ready to hold court.

A MAN TO WATCH — General Santa Anna seems to have been more successful as a con man than he was at leading an army.

After the Texas patriots under General Sam Houston defeated the Mexicans at San Jacinto, Santa Anna returned to Mexico and eventually became that country's dictator. Ousted in 1855, he went into exile and eventually showed up in New York. Fascinated by the suave general, New Yorkers eagerly purchased $750,000 worth of first mortgage bonds which Santa Anna promised to redeem in 1868 and which were secured by his "palaces and grounds" in Mexico.

Once he had the Yankee money in hand, however, he disappeared. He died in 1876, blind, broke and almost forgotten, without ever repaying the money.

Women Are People, Too

FIRST STRIPPER — A Texas beauty introduced the "strip tease" to the stage a little over a century ago.

She was Adah Menken, a native of Tennessee, who grew up in the East Texas town of Nacogdoches. As a young girl, she ran away with an actor in a touring troupe and launched a career that was to make her world-famous as the first actress to perform "in the nude."

The play was "Mazeppa" and it opened on Broadway June 3, 1860. Cast in the title role, Adah was called upon to strip to apparent nudity and ride a horse off the stage. Actually, she wore skin-colored tights from neck to ankles, but the deception was so good that the play became a great hit.

FASHION NOTE — Long before Messrs. Neiman and Marcus ever thought about opening their exclusive shops, Texas women believed in wearing expensive clothes if the occasion warranted. On January 31, 1899, the daughter of a Denison bank official wore a $35,000 dress to a church social!

Miss Bertie Oldham decided to ornament her dress that evening with $15,000 worth of $20, $100 and $1,000 bills, topped by a hat trimmed with $1,000 bills and garnished with $20,000 worth of borrowed diamonds.

This caused a Denison newspaper to comment that "disrobing her after the party was something of an auditing achievement."

NO DETERGENTS, EITHER — Water was so scarce in the early days that ranch wives made every drop assigned to cleaning do three jobs.

Clothes were washed in it first. Next, the children were bathed in it. Finally, the suds remaining were used to scrub the floors.

CIRCUS QUEEN — From 1869 to 1918, one of the most popular shows in Texas was Mollie Bailey's Circus.

The only major show of its kind ever operated in the state by a woman, the Mollie A. Bailey Circus boasted 31 painted wagons, 170 head of trained circus stock, a small menagerie and a troupe of acrobats. Mollie was both the manager and the star of the show, and when she died in 1918, the show died with her.

WHO WAS TEXAS' "BETSY ROSS"? — Almost a century and a half after the Third Congress of the Republic of Texas adopted the Lone Star Flag as the ensign of the new nation, historians still aren't sure who designed it.

Joanna Troutman, an 18-year-old Knoxville, Ga., girl usually is credited with making the first flag. Other evidence, however, indicates that Mrs. Sarah Bradley Dodson, wife of a lieutenant in the Texas revolutionary army, may have designed the red and white banner with a single star on a field of blue.

Both women did make emblems that were carried in battle during the Texas revolution against Mexico. The probability is that the symbol finally adopted as the Lone Star Flag incorporated the designs of both.

STRANGE LADY — Elisabet Ney, the beautiful, head-strong German girl who became Texas' first eminent sculptress, was regarded by her contemporaries as an oddball — and with good reason.

Although married to Dr. Edmund Montgomery, she lived with him only occasionally and never used his name. When one of their two sons died while they were living at Liendo Plantation in Waller County, Miss Ney cremated the body in the living room fire place.

SPY IN PETTICOATS — Houston's Washington Cemetery is the burial place of the only woman soldier ever recognized by the Federal Army during the Civil War.

Her name was Emma Seelye. But from May 17, 1861, until April, 1863, she was "Private Frank Thompson," first a "male" nurse in a field hospital, later postmaster for a brigade, and finally a trusted spy.

After contracting malaria during spy missions behind the Confederate lines, "Frank Thompson" requested a furlough.

When leave was denied, Private Thompson deserted and emerged shortly after as Emma Edmonds. Her real identity wasn't revealed until she published a book, "Nurse and Spy."

Later, Emma married a man named Linus Seelye. In 1893, they moved to La Porte, Texas, to be near a son and his family. Emma died there in 1898. She was reburied in Houston in 1901, and her grave is still carefully tended by the descendants of the Grand Army of the Republic.

IT COULD ONLY HAPPEN HERE — When the Julian Bivins Museum was opened in the one-time courthouse at Old Tascosa in the Panhandle, Mrs. Neal Johnson was asked to do the honors by snipping the ceremonial ribbon.

Disdaining to use the pair of dainty scissors handed to her, Mrs. Johnson picked up a bull-whip, backed off and expertly severed the ribbon.

HISTORICAL HUMBUG — It isn't true that Governor James Stephen Hogg had two daughters whom he named Ima and Ura as a joke. His only daughter is named Ima, but her father saw nothing amusing about it.

He named her Ima after the heroine in a Civil War narrative poem written by his brother, Tom. In naming the daughter, whom he often called "the sunshine of my household," Governor Hogg intended no pun.

CORRECTING THE HISTORIANS — Mrs. Jane Long, the "Mother of Texas," usually is cited as the first known woman of English descent to bear a child in Texas. She wasn't.

The honor goes to Mrs. Jack Dill, who moved to Texas with her husband and four children in 1793. She gave birth to a daughter, Helena, in Nacogdoches on September 8, 1804. Jane Long's child was not born until December 21, 1821.

Actually, Mrs. Dill may not have been the mother of the first white child born in Texas, either. There were many settlers who came to Texas in the late 1790's, and some probably had children after they arrived. The Dill child, however, is the first for whom birth records exist.

THEY STARTED HERE — Neither the miniskirt nor the topless bathing suit is new to Texas.

In "Commerce of the Prairies," published in 1844, Josiah Gregg wrote that women of the Waco, Wichita and other Indian tribes went about with breasts bare. He said that "their only gown consists of about a yard and a half of cloth or else a small, dressed skin suspended from the waist."

IT'S A WOMAN'S WORLD — Women who attended early-day coeducational schools in Texas got the same education that was given to men — but they weren't graduated with the same degrees.

Waco University (now Baylor) became the first coeducational school when it opened its doors to women in 1865. It conferred the standard Bachelor of Arts degree on men — but gave women one called the Mistress of Arts.

Andrew Female College, which closed its doors long ago, at first conferred the degree of Graduate of the College on women. Later it changed this to a Mistress of Polite Literature degree.

MADAM JUSTICE — For one short period, every judge on the Supreme Court of Texas was a woman.

In 1925, the male judges of the court disqualified themselves to hear a case. Governor Pat M. Neff then appointed Mrs. Hortense Ward as a special chief justice and Ruth Virginia Brazzil and Hattie L. Henenberg as special associate justices to hear the case. Once their verdict was in, the regular judges returned to the bench.

FOR LADIES ONLY — Many early-day Texas post offices were built with separate entrances for women.

Since many pioneer post offices were a favorite hangout for the town loafers, some postmasters thought the separate entrances were advisable.

THE TEXAS TORNADO — Carry Nation, the hatchet-packing foe of tobacco and booze, ran a hotel in Richmond, Texas, before moving to Kansas to launch her career as a saloon-wrecker. career as a saloon-wrecker.

One night in the 1880's the town of Richmond caught fire. The blaze, aided by a strong wind, bore down on her hotel, but Carry refused to let the volunteer fire-fighters remove any of her furniture. The fire, she assured them, would never touch her property.

It didn't. After destroying nearby buildings, the flames miraculously stopped at Carry's property line. It was, she said, her first victory over the devil.

THE CURSE OF SAN PATRICIO — When the citizens of San Patricio hanged Chipita Rodriguez from a mesquite tree more than a century ago, they also signed the death warrant for their town.

Chipita Rodriguez was a woman — the only one ever hanged in Texas — and the evidence suggests that she wasn't guilty of the murder with which she was charged. But a jury said she was, and Judge Benjamin Neal sentenced her to die. The sentence was carried out on November 13, 1863, with most of the 1,000 townspeople looking on.

From that day forward, however, San Patricio itself began to die. In a few years, the county seat was moved to Sinton. By 1920, the post office was closed. Today San Patricio is a ghost town, made so (say old-timers) because its citizens hanged an innocent woman.

HAPPY WITHOUT HUSBANDS — If a Texas housewife tired of her husband in the 1870's but couldn't — or wouldn't — divorce him, she could shed him by joining the Sanctificationist Sisters of Belton.

The Sanctificationists began as a religious order when Mrs. Martha McWhirter heard a "Voice from Heaven" as she washed her breakfast dishes. Under the rules of the order she founded, any woman thus sanctified could leave her "unsanctified" husband.

Many did, and for more than 30 years, the Sanctificationists flourished. The Sisters put all of their earnings into a common fund and shared all their belongings. They sold "sanctified" butter and milk, operated a laundry, sold stove wood, nursed, worked as servants and, in 1891, began operating a successful Bell County hotel.

Husbands fumed, and one or two became "sanctified" and joined. However, the Sanctificationists remained primarily a feminist organization until it finally died a natural death early in this century.

SPOUSE DIVIDERS — If a married woman in early Texas decided that she wanted a new husband and the courts were tardy in granting a divorce, she could appeal directly to the Congress — especially if her new love was a Congressman.

In 1838, Mrs. Sophia Aughinbaugh decided to shed her husband and marry Holland Coffee, a member of the Third Congress of the Republic. The Harris County court was slow in acting on her petition, however, and she appealed directly to the Congress.

Her plea was dutifully passed to a committee, was favorably reported out and, on January 15, 1839, "the Senate and House of Representatives of the Republic of Texas in Congress assembled" ruled that Mrs. Aughinbaugh was legally divorced. She married Congressman Coffee a month later.

IT TAKES ALL KINDS — Mrs. Grover Damuth, the 1968 "Mrs. Texas," started toward her title astride a horse.

In 1952, she and Grover Damuth were on matching white horses when they were married at a Tomball rodeo. The minister and 15 members of the wedding party also were on horseback while 5,000 rodeo fans watched the ceremony.

Black Gold

THE DAY THE EARTH FELL IN — What happens when oil wells suck all of that black gold out of the ground? Sometimes the earth falls in.

It happened on October 9, 1929, when a multi-million-dollar oil field in Hardin County suddenly began sinking. By the end of the day, a five-acre tract had settled 30 feet below ground level. Within two days, the five acres were 100 feet below their previous level and oil and water poured in to form a lake.

"Cavity Lake" may still be seen near the town of Sourlake.

FOOTNOTE TO HISTORY — From August 17, 1931, until December, 1932, the giant East Texas oil field was allowed to operate only under the watchful eye of armed National Guardsmen.

The "war" between the oil producers and the state resulted over the efforts of the Railroad Commission to limit the production of crude petroleum. To stabilize prices and conserve the oil reserves, the Commission ordered production limited to 90,000 barrels per day. Most producers ignored the order. Records show that on the day before the troops were sent in, the field produced 848,000 barrels — almost ten times more than the legal limit.

Once Governor Ross S. Sterling declared martial law and the National Guard took over the field, production was rolled back. Some operators, however, continued to flout the proration order and to produce and sell surreptitiously what came to be known as "hot oil."

After 16 months of martial law, the troops were withdrawn just before Christmas, 1932, when a Federal court ruled that Governor Sterling had acted illegally. But the "oil war" was a success in that it brought about conservation laws that now protect both the industry and the state.

IT'S EVERYWHERE — In oil-rich East Texas, the black gold is where you find it.

Tourists visiting Gladewater, in Gregg County, for the first time are startled by the sight of oil derricks interspersed among the tombstones in Rosedale Cemetery. It's probably the only cemetery in the world where the thud-thud of electric pumps at operating oil wells provide an unusual requiem for graveside services.

THE BOY WITH THE X-RAY EYES — Guy Fenley, as a 13-year-old sixth grader, is credited with "discovering" one of Texas' greatest oil fields by using his uncanny ability to "see" through the ground.

As a youngster of eight, Fenley discovered that he could locate underground water through some sort of unusual vision. Farmers and ranchers in his native Zavala County gladly paid to have "the boy with the x-ray eyes" tell them where to dig their wells. The youth never failed.

In 1901, when a Uvalde oil company purchased some leases at Spindletop, near Beaumont, Guy Fenley was taken there to see if his strange powers also included finding oil. They did, and he picked almost the exact spot where the great gusher, Spindletop No. 1, later was brought in,

Mr. Fenley, who died a few years ago at La Pryor, always felt that he had a God-given gift which would be spoiled by selling it. It was. When his father began selling his services, Guy began to lose his strange vision. Throughout his adult life, he was never able to find either oil or water again.

TRAVELING TEXAS — One of the state's most unusual parks honors the old-timers who drilled its early oil fields.

Known as Joe Roughneck Park (because drillers and tool-pushers were called "roughnecks"), the park is on State Highway 64 two miles from Turnertown, in Rusk County. A bronze bust set on a piece of drill pipe represents all of that special breed of oil field workers.

The park also has a wooden derrick like that used in the boom days. Old-time rig carpenters came out of retirement to build it.

BELIEVE-IT-OR-NOT — There's an oil field southeast of Palestine so rich in the stuff that the blue-black liquid gold literally melts and runs out when a sample of the same is laid in the hot summer sun.

However, the field hasn't made anybody rich.

Discovered in 1935, the Camp Hill field appeared to be a wildcatter's dream. Only 450 feet below the surface is an estimated 50 million barrels of some of the best grade oil ever found anywhere in the world.

The oil is so thick and heavy that it doesn't gush out of the ground. It oozes — and that's the problem. Thus far, nobody has been able to devise a pump or any other system that can successfully get the oil to the surface in large enough quantities to make marketing it very profitable.

ALL THAT GLITTERS — Only one out of every nine oil wells is a financial success.

To be profitable, a well must supply a million barrels of oil or a billion cubic feet of natural gas for sale. Eight out of nine wells fall short.

THE NEW MAN BEHIND THE STAR — Texas has a two-man private police force whose only job is to stop thieves from rustling pipe, drill bits and even derricks from oil fields.

Oil-field thieves swipe everything from the mercury in gas meters on well sites to tools. One gang actually stole a 129-foot derrick, including the engines and tons of tools.

Stopping such thefts is the job of two former sheriffs who are the private police force of the Texas Mid-Continent Oil and Gas Association.

LEGENDS THAT LIVE — After the McClesky No. 1 spudded in on October 21, 1917, and turned Ranger into a boom town, speculators tried to buy up the rights to drill everywhere in Eastland County.

One group, so legend says, even offered $100,000 to the Baptist Church at nearby Merriam for the right to drill on its cemetery. A nameless local poet preserved the church's answer in these words:

> All of the oildom knew the answer,
> When the chairman shook his head.
> Pointing past the men of millions
> At the city of the dead.
> 'Why disturb the weary tenants
> In yon narrow strip of sod?
> 'Tis not ours, but theirs —
> The title vested by the will of God.
> We, the Board, have talked it over,
> Pro and con without avail.
> We rejected your hungred thousand —
> Merriam is not for sale.'

OIL TOWN — Houston is headquarters for more oil companies than any city in the nation outside of New York.

NO MONEY IN OIL — Pennsylvania experts once decided that Texas oil wasn't worth the effort.

In 1866, Lynis T. Barrett brought in Texas' first producing oil well at Melrose, Nacogdoches County. He took samples to Pennsylvania where the first oil well in the U.S. had been brought in seven years before. When John F. Carll, the Pennsylvania Petroleum expert, saw the Texas sample, he contracted to develop the Nacogdoches field.

After some second thought, however, the Pennsylvanian decided that the Texas development wouldn't be worth the cost and cancelled his contract. Less than a year later, a second well was brought in at Oil Springs and Texas' first oil boom was launched anyway.

GAS, ANYONE? — It takes 18 pages in the Odessa telephone directory just to list the oil exploration and oil service industries located in that city of 95,000 people.

SHALL WE GATHER AT THE GUSHER? — Hymns used to help usher in new wells at the great Mexia oil field during the 1920's.

Albert E. Humphreys, one of the developers of the Limestone County field, used to hire a Negro choir to sing spirituals around a new well that was about to be spudded in.

TEXAS FACT — Who said oil was a comparatively new industry in Texas? In 1543, the explorer De Soto used Texas oil to patch his boats. Actually, the material he used was a kind of petroleum base asphalt.

MUD IN YOUR EYE — In Houston, about 1,500 people earn their living making mud.

Houston's mud-makers annually sell more than $100 million worth of the stuff to oil companies around the world. It's used for such varied things as cooling drill pipes and putting out oil well fires.

SAINT OF THE IMPOSSIBLE — Santa Rita, the discovery well that launched the great Permian Basin oil field in West Texas, was so named because two devout women wanted to honor their patron saint.

The ladies, both New Yorkers, told promoter Frank Pickrell that they would back his search for oil only if he would name his well after the "Saint of the Impossible." He agreed and, in August, 1921, climbed atop the rig and christened the well with rose petals that had been blessed by a priest.

Santa Rita lived up to her name and produced the impossible. Less than two years later, the well blew in as a gusher and opened up one of the greatest oil strikes in U.S. history.

Events That
Shaped History

GOATS OF THE DEVIL — A unique chapter of Texas history is folded away in the ruins of Camp Verde, in Kerr County. It is the story of how the camel got the Army mule's job, then lost it again.

In 1854, when Secretary of War Jefferson Davis got Congress to appropriate $30,000 so the Army could experiment with camels as beasts of burden, Camp Verde was selected as the training site for the imported beasts which the Comanche Indians called "goats of the devil." From 1854 until the Civil War, Camp Verde camels roamed the West, packing supplies to California, helping to survey the Big Bend of Texas and performing a thousand tasks.

Failure of the Congress to appropriate more funds, plus the beginning of the Civil War, ended the strange experiment to find a pack animal that could replace the mule. By 1869, Camp Verde, "home of the camels," had been deactivated.

On March 26, 1919, fire destroyed most of what still remained of the camp. However, one of the old adobe quarters used by Camp Verde officers has been reconstructed as a ranch home. The visitor who looks carefully can still find the rock outlines of the old camel caravanserai.

FIRST CAPITAL WAS IN LOUISIANA — Texas' first capital was located in Louisiana, near the present town of Robeline in the land of the Adaes Indians!

Its founder was Louis Juchereau St. Denis, a French officer who had left Mobile in 1713 to promote trade between the French and the Spanish. En route to Texas, he founded Natchitoches, the first settlement in Louisiana.

After arriving at Presidio del Norte on the Rio Grande, he met and married Manuela de Sanchez Ramon, granddaughter of the post commander, and decided to throw in his lot with the Spanish. In 1717, he guided a Spanish expedition back toward Natchitoches to promote trade with the French. At Robeline, only 12 miles from the French post, he stopped and built the Mission San Miguel de Linares de los Adaes.

Ironically, this Spanish post, which was designed to prevent further French expansion to the west, owed its founding to a Frenchman.

In 1719, war broke out between France and Spain. The commander of the Natchitoches post attacked Los Adaes and the Spanish abandoned the mission. Two years later, the Spanish returned, rebuilt the mission, added a fort and named it the headquarters and capital of Texas.

It remained so until it was abandoned in 1733 and San Antonio de Bexar became the new capital.

THE TROOP SHIP OF SAN JACINTO — Texas might have lost its fight for independence from Mexico if it hadn't been for Captain J. E. Ross who commanded a tiny, wood-burning steamboat named the *Yellowstone*.

In April, 1835, General Sam Houston's pursuit of the Mexican Army came to a halt when he reached the flooding Brazos River near Groce's Ferry. For 12 days, the Texians camped on the river bank, unable to get men and supplies across. Then Houston learned that the *Yellowstone* was at Washington, just six miles up the river.

He sent a messenger to Captain Ross promising each crew member "one third of a league of land" if he would use the *Yellowstone* to transport the Texian Army and supplies across the river. Ross responded, hauling more than 700 men, 200 horses and other supplies across the swollen Brazos by nightfall on April 13. Eight days later, Houston got to San Jacinto and defeated Santa Anna.

Again the *Yellowstone* was pressed into service, first to bring President David G. Burnet and his cabinet from Galveston to the battlefield and then to take them (along with Houston and his Mexican prisoners) to Velasco to sign the treaty of peace.

For their help in winning the war, neither the owners of the *Yellowstone* nor its officers and crew ever received any payment from Texas — an oversight that Houston tried to rectify until his death.

THE LAW THAT MADE DALLAS A CITY — A free-flowing spring and a unique act of the Legislature helped

make a hamlet named Dallas the second largest city in Texas.

In the 1870's, when the Texas & Pacific Railway was building westward across Texas, its destination was Fort Worth. Nobody objected to the proposed route. However, John H. Cochran, who represented Dallas in the Legislature, did introduce a peculiar bill. It specified that the T. & P. would lose its state land grants unless its railroad crossed the recently completed north-south line of the Houston & Texas Central "within one mile of Browder Springs."

Other legislators, anxious to please the citizens of Browder Springs, passed the bill. They didn't seem to be aware that Browder Springs was not a town. It was, as Cochran well knew, only the name of the spring in the heart of Dallas that supplied all of the water for that hamlet of 1,500 people.

By requiring that the railroads cross "within a mile of Browder Springs," Cochran thus guaranteed that Dallas would become a transportation crossroads.

THE DEVIL'S NECKLACE — History credits an Illinois farmer named Joseph F. Glidden with the invention of barbed wire. However, a Texan was making and using "the devil's necklace" 17 years before Glidden patented the idea.

He was John Grinninger (or Grenniger), a European immigrant who worked for an Austin iron foundry. Grinninger had a small truck garden on Waller Creek near what is now the capital city's Town Lake.

To protect his garden, Grinninger strung two wires along the top of the fence surrounding his plot. These wires were twisted together with bits of hoop iron. Between the pieces of hoop iron, Grinninger placed sharpened pieces of wire with points projecting up and down.

Grinninger never tried to sell his idea, however. In 1862, he was murdered in Austin. Five years later, in 1867, the first patent on barbed wire was issued. Then, in 1874, Glidden patented his wire and founded a new industry.

NO WHIPPED CREAM? — Denison, Grayson County, claims to be the birthplace of the ice cream soda.

One day in 1873, J. A. Euper, who operated the only non-alcoholic oasis in town at the time, was experimenting with his new $800 soda fountain made of fancy Italian marble. Accidentally, he squirted carbonated water over a dish of ice cream. Hoping to salvage what seemed to be a loss, he added some chocolate syrup.

The result was so satisfying that he began serving the concoction to all customers as a gimmick — and thus a new confection was born.

NON-UNION MAN — A husband-wife spat kept Texas' decision to become one of the United States from being unanimous.

When the delegates gathered in Austin in 1845 to vote on the invitation to statehood extended by the U.S. government, Richard Bache of Galveston was the only delegate to vote "no."

Actually, Bache (who was a grandson of Benjamin Franklin) wanted to see Texas become a state. However, he and his wife were estranged and she happened to be the sister of George M. Dallas, the vice-president of the United States.

Bache was so embittered against his wife that he refused to vote to bring Texas into the Union so long as a member of her family had anything to do with the administration of the country.

TEETOTALLER'S TOWN — Saint Jo, in Montague County, got its name because one of its founders had a thing about drinking alcoholic beverages.

The townsite was laid out in 1873 by Captain I. H. Boggess and his partner, Joe Howell. Legend has it that Boggess, who liked his liquor, did the actual surveying of the site after he had belted down a few drinks. As a result, the town's streets do not run exactly north and south or east and west as Boggess intended they should.

At any rate, Boggess built the Stonewall Saloon (now restored) as the town's first permanent building. Joe Howell expressed his displeasure at his partner's profiting from strong drink and asked Boggess what he planned to name his sinful town.

Boggess thought the question over, looked at his partner and replied: "Since you're so high-minded, I think we ought to name it after you. We'll call it Saint Joe." It's still named that — without the final "e."

LOVE LETTER TO A NEW FATHERLAND — Friedrich Ernst, a reluctant pioneer himself, was more responsible than any other man for the beginning of German settlements in Texas.

Ernst came to Texas with his family in 1831. That first winter was harsh and the family almost starved to death. Nevertheless, Ernst fell in love with Texas and wrote a glowing letter about the new land to a friend in Oldenburg.

The letter made Texas sound like such a Promised Land that the friend had it published in an Oldenburg paper. It was picked up and reprinted by other papers throughout Germany. Lured by Ernst's letter, hundreds of Germans began moving to Texas. Today their descendants can still be found in the more than a dozen communities they established in the state.

Ernst, who had been a gardener in his native Oldenburg, was reluctant, gun-shy pioneer who lacked most of the skills required on the frontier. He discovered that he could raise fine tobacco on the land he received as a member of Stephen F. Austin's colony. To find a market for it, he decided to lay out a town, bring in other German settlers and provide them with jobs in a cigar factory.

The town of Industry, Austin County, was the result.

VALLEY OF HEROES — Three Presidents of the United States, the President of the Confederacy and at least 14 generals learned their first lessons in commanding men while stationed in the Rio Grande Valley of Texas.

Zachary Taylor, Franklin Pierce and Ulysses S. Grant all served in the Rio Grande Valley sometime between 1845 and the beginning of the Civil War. So did Jefferson Davis and Robert E. Lee.

Others who received some of their earliest combat experience in the Brownsville area include Generals Meade, Pickett, Stonewall Jackson, Bragg, Longstreet, Beauregard, Albert Sidney Johnston, Joseph E. A. Johnston, Sherman, McClellan, Phil Sheridan and Joe Hooker.

THE 'X' THAT KILLED A CITY — In the register of Jefferson's old Excelsior House there's a scrawled, but still legible, century-old prophecy that reads: "The end of Jefferson, Texas X."

Citizens of the bustling river port laughed when Jay Gould, the railroad magnate, wrote those words in 1872. Jefferson then had a population of 30,000 and more than 200 river steamers unloaded annually at its docks. The citizens were confident that nothing could hurt the profitable river traffic, so when Gould offered to locate his railroad shops there in exchange for free right-of-way, they turned him down.

Angered, Gould decided to wipe Jefferson off the map and his entry in the hotel register was a warning. He located his shops at nearby Marshall, designed his railroad to bypass Jefferson and, within a decade, reduced the former "Queen City of Texas" to a sleepy hamlet.

THE LIGHT THAT FAILED — By stealing the lenses from the Port Isabel lighthouse in 1863, Col. John S. (Rip) Ford may have helped to prolong the Civil War.

After Ford stole the light, visible for 16 miles, Federal vessels were hampered in enforcing the blockade of Southern ports. Confederate blockade runners, however, were familiar with the Gulf waters and easily slipped their cargoes of cotton, worth a dollar a pound in Europe, past the patrol boats.

Sale of the cotton bolstered the South's economy and kept the conflict alive long after it should have ended.

THE TASTE OF TEXAS IN FRENCH WINE — If there's a slight Texas flavor in a glass of champagne or burgundy, there's a reason. The French wine industry owes its life to Texas.

In the late 1890's, grape production throughout France was threatened by a root disease known as phylloxera. After every known remedy had been tried without success, the French government appealed to T. V. Munson of Denison. Munson had become famous in horticultural circles by developing vast vineyards through the crossbreeding of native Red River Valley grapes.

Using the native Texas grapes, he was able to breed a variety that resisted the disease which was wiping out the wine industry in France. Eventually every French vineyard was regrafted with the new variety developed in Texas, and the industry was saved.

A grateful France conferred the Legion of Honor, its highest reward, on the small-town Texas nurseryman who had saved French wines for the gourmets of the world.

FOOTNOTE TO HISTORY — The assassination of President John F. Kennedy in Dallas November 22, 1963, was not the first time that a visit to that city by a U.S. president has resulted in tragedy.

On October 23, 1909, President William Howard Taft was being driven through downtown Dallas in an automobile caravan. At a street intersection, an excited spectator tried to break through a cordon of militia to get a closer look at the President. He was bayoneted to death.

STATEHOOD BY A SINGLE VOTE — Texas owes its statehood to an unknown grain miller in DeKalb County, Indiana.

It was election day in 1844 and the miller had already decided that he would be too busy to vote. On the way to his mill, however, friends stopped him and urged him to cast his ballot first. He did, and when the ballots were counted, the winning candidate had a margin of a single vote — the one the miller had cast.

The successful candidate was U.S. Senator Edward Allen Hannegan. He happened to be presiding when the question of statehood for Texas came to a vote before the Senate. The result was a tie, but Senator Hannegan, from the chair, cast the deciding vote in favor of admitting Texas to the Union.

THE REPUBLIC THAT HISTORY FORGOT — The first Texas Republic was established in 1812, 24 years before the Declaration of Independence was framed and issued at Washington-on-the-Brazos.

It was the brainchild of Jose Bernardo Maximiliano Gutierrez de Lara, a Mexican rebel. He was aided by Augustus William Magee, a West Point graduate who resigned from the U.S. Army to help. Their plan was to invade Texas and liberate it from Spanish rule.

Their motley army moved across the Sabine in August, 1812, capturing Nacogdoches, Trinidad, La Bahia and San Antonio. They issued a declaration of independence, wrote a constitution and designed a solid green flag as their standard. For a short time they governed Texas, naming it the Republic of the West.

However, De Lara was deposed as leader of the insurgents, Magee died and, on August 18, 1813, the revolutionaries were defeated and routed at the Battle of the Medina River. Thus died the first Republic of Texas.

THE CITIZEN WHO FINANCED INDEPEN-DENCE — Texas financed the Battle of San Jacinto with a loan from the personal fortune of a single patriot.

He was James Hamilton, former governor of South Carolina, who loaned the provisional government of the Republic of Texas $210,000 in 1836. His only security was scrip to be exchanged for public lands if the debt wasn't repaid.

It was not. Once independence from Mexico was won, the new Republic was broke. For 21 years, Hamilton tried to collect the debt Texas owed him, but failed.

In 1857, the Texas Legislature finally invited Hamilton to come to Austin to discuss "an adjustment." However, the ship on which he was traveling from New Orleans to Galveston sank and Hamilton was drowned.

Two months later, Texas "repaid" its debt by naming a new county Hamilton in honor of "his services to the Republic."

VOLUNTEERS WHO DIDN'T — Although Colonel William Barret Travis, commander of the Alamo, called for help clearly and often, only 32 Texans ever heeded his call.

Of these, 30 were from one town — Gonzales. They left their homes on the afternoon of February 27, 1836, were joined on the march by two others and finally got inside the Alamo at 3 a.m. on March 1. Five days later, they died.

At least one other group tried to reach the Alamo in time to help, but failed. So it was that the "immortal 32" became the first, and only, reinforcements to come to the aid of Travis.

THE SECOND BATTLE OF SAN JACINTO — Getting title to the 440 acres of real estate where General Sam Houston won Texas its freedom from Mexico April 21, 1836, was a battle almost as rugged as the original.

In 1891, the Daughters of the Republic of Texas decided that Texas should acquire the San Jacinto Battleground, site of one of the most decisive confrontations in history. The organization petitioned the 23rd Legislature to appropriate $75,000 to buy the land and erect a suitable monument.

The Legislature whittled the appropriation to $15,000 and Governor James Stephen Hogg vetoed even that amount. He suggested that he might approve $750 to purchase a strip of the land on Buffalo Bayou and the Legislature approved. But the governor failed to appoint anyone to make the purchase and the money was never used.

In 1894, the Daughters held a bazaar that netted them $721.15 as a start. Three years later, they brought the governor and the entire 25th Legislature to the battleground and entertained them at a picnic and dance. The lawmakers returned to Austin and appropriated $10,000 for the purchase.

In 1900, the San Jacinto Battleground finally was purchased. It was not until 1939, however, that the monument — the highest masonry structure in the world — was completed.

POUND THOSE RAILS! — One of the great railroad construction feats occurred July 29, 1894, when the Southern Pacific changed all 232 miles of its Houston-Shreveport line from narrow to standard gauge track in one day!

For six weeks before the widening took place, section laborers replaced every six-foot cross-tie with eight-footers. Crews also widened every bridge. By the target date for the change in gauge, only the rail itself had to be replaced.

To do the job, the railroad hired 1,000 convicts from the Texas prison. They were assembled into 32 groups of 25 men each and four gangs of 50 men each. The smaller crews were placed six miles apart and the larger gangs 13 miles apart.

Work began at daybreak on the sidings and switches. At 8 a.m. the regularly scheduled trains left each end of the main line headed for the opposite terminals of Houston and Shreveport. They passed midway along the route. As the last cars passed, the crews began replacing the rail and completed the job (except for permanent spiking) by nightfall.

Tales Of
The Towns

THE CITY BUILT BY GHOSTS — Port Arthur (pop. 57,500) may be America's most authentic ghost town.

Its founder, Arthur Edward Stilwell, was a hard-headed, successful businessman, but he had believed in phantoms since childhood. His "Brownies," as he called them, came to him in dreams, foretelling events that didn't happen until years later.

When he was building his Kansas City Southern Railway in the 1890's and looking for a terminus on the Gulf, the "Brownies" warned him to by-pass Galveston and build his city on a Sabine Lake swamp. He took their advice, bought 40,000 acres of swamp land for less than $300,000 and named the place Port Arthur.

The ghosts were right. In 1900, Galveston was all but destroyed by a hurricane and flood. And a year later, the Spindletop Oil Field blew in and made Port Arthur a world port.

GOD'S LITTLE ACREAGE — The Lord God of Israel once was the sole owner of a 144-acre plot in the piney woods of Polk County.

As might be expected, this unusual real estate was the "promised land" — at least that's what it was termed by a Canadian named A. M. Turnbull who came to Texas in 1890 looking for a Utopia he had seen in a vision. He sought a land to be settled by a religious sect known as the "Flying Roll," which called itself one of the lost tribes of Israel.

Turnbull found his promised land between Livingston and Leggett — 144 square acres owned by Mr. and Mrs. Joseph

Peebles. He converted the Peebles as followers of his sect and they gave him their land. Turnbull then deeded it to God — an act duly recorded at the Polk County courthouse.

The plot was named "Israel" and Turnbull announced that he would seek 144,000 pilgrims to settle it. Eventually about 200 homes were built by members who let their hair and beards grow and who strictly observed the laws of Moses. Each January 14, door posts of the church were anointed and the members ate unleavened bread. And each July 5 — "Jubilee Day" — was spent in fasting.

HOW IT BEGAN — Fort Worth's famous slogan, "Where the West Begins," predated the founding of the town by six years.

In 1843, General Edward H. Tarrant and Captain Edward S. Terrell negotiated a treaty with the Indians stipulating that the tribes were to remain west of a line that was traced through the future site of Fort Worth. Thus, when Major Ripley A. Arnold founded Fort Worth on June 6, 1849, his new town literally was located on the line "where the West begins."

TOWN OF SEVEN FOUNDERS — Newport, Clay County, was named only after a long and bitter squabble by the residents over what the community should be called.

When an acceptable name seemed impossible to find, one citizen discovered that the initial letters of the last names of the seven men who had founded the town — Norman, Ezell, Welch, Pruitt, Owsley, Reiger and Turner — spelled "Newport." And Newport it became.

SOME CHANGES WERE MADE — A settlement that began as a collection of saloons and houses of prostitution ended up being named for a saint!

In the late 1860's, a settlement was started across the Concho River from old Fort Concho. Established primarily to serve the needs of the soldiers for a place to carouse, it was called Over-the-River. Later is was renamed Santa Angela and still later changed by the Post Office Department to San Angelo.

THEY NEEDED IT — In the 1890's, residents of a new Stephens County community petitioned Washington that a post office was a "necessity."

In the manner peculiar to bureaucrats, Washington granted the petition and named the post office "Necessity."

FIDDLERS FREE — San Antonio citizens were so anxious for their offspring to become musicians that the city schools began offering free violin lessons to all comers in 1853.

IRISH BRIGADOON — San Patricio, once a thriving community 30 miles up the Nueces River from Corpus Christi, today is almost a ghost town that only comes alive on St. Patrick's Day.

Founded by Irish immigrants in 1831 as San Patricio de Hibernia (Spanish for St. Patrick of Ireland), it is remembered in history only because its citizens hanged Chipita Rodriguez, the only woman ever to be executed in this manner in Texas. Legend says that after Chipita was hanged on November 13, 1863, for a crime which she probably didn't commit, the town began to die.

It comes to life, however, each St. Patrick's Day as thousands of descendants of the Irish colonists gather in the old town and celebrate the day of their patron saint. After 24 hours, San Patricio becomes a ghost town again.

BUFFALO TOWN — Snyder, the bustling Scurry County seat, was first called "Hide Town" because so many of its structures were made of buffalo hides.

A local waterway, Deep Creek, became a popular campsite for buffalo hunters in the 1870's. So many camped along the creek that a Dutch trader named W. H. (Pete) Snyder decided to establish a trading post on its banks and the town grew from that beginning. It is named, of course, for the enterprising merchant.

NO GIRLS ALLOWED — Bull Creek, Scurry County, was so named because it was a favorite watering place for male bison. For some reason, herds of buffalo that gathered there never included either cows or calves.

SEEING DOUBLE IN DALLAS — Texas used to have a couple of twin towns named Dallas.

John Neely Bryan's original Dallas already was a going concern in 1872 when the Houston & Texas Central Railroad whistled in. However, the railroad built its station on land it owned about a mile east of the present Dallas County courthouse and proclaimed a new town of East Dallas.

For the next 18 years, East Dallas flourished alongside Dallas and once claimed a population of 15,000. In 1889, however, the Legislature passed a bill repealing the East Dallas charter and incorporating it into the larger city of Dallas.

Nobody in East Dallas objected and it made the citizens of Big D positively delirious when the two became one on January 4, 1890. The reason: The combined population of 38,067 made Dallas the biggest city in Texas.

GOOFY GEOGRAPHY — If some Starr County citizens are confused about where to get their mail, there's a reason.

The Santa Elena post office is not in Santa Elena at all, but is four miles away in La Gloria.

It all began when the Santa Elena postmistress gave her hand in marriage to a bachelor in La Gloria. When she moved to her husband's home, she brought her post office with her. She even moved the building and the sign.

That's why the highway signs tell the traveler that he's in La Gloria, but the sign on the only Federal building in town reads: "U.S. Post Office, Santa Elena, Texas."

THE TOWN TOBACCO BUILT — Industry, Austin County, was the first German town in Texas. It was founded in 1838 by Friedrich Ernst because he needed labor for a cigar factory he wanted to open.

Ernst, who had been a gardener in his native Oldenburg, was a reluctant, gun-shy pioneer who lacked most of the skills required on the frontier. He discovered that he could raise fine tobacco on the land he received as a member of Stephen F. Austin's colony. To find a market for it, he decided to lay out a town, bring in other German settlers and provide them with jobs in a cigar factory.

The town of Industry was the result, but many other German settlements were to follow. Ernst's letters to friends back home gave such glowing accounts of life in Texas that he is credited with starting the first real migration of Germans to the new land.

UNCERTAINTY IN UNCERTAIN — Postal authorities aren't certain about Uncertain.

They've closed the post office again at the Harrison County resort community near Marshall which boasts the unusual name. But Uncertain residents aren't worried because they've never been certain about the status of their post office.

After Uncertain was established as a Caddo Lake resort, it had a post office for some years. Then the government closed it. Then they reopened it. Now it's closed again, and Uncertain isn't certain that it will ever be reopened.

TWO-NAME TOWN — Hermleigh, in Scurry County, has had its ups and downs over what to call itself.

Because R. C. Herm and Harry W. Harlin gave land in 1907 on which to locate the town, the citizens asked the post office to name it "Hermlin" to honor both. Washington authorities refused and changed it to Hermleigh.

During World War I, however, local patriots decided that a name with German origins wasn't proper and petitioned Washington to rename the town Foch after the famous French general. The change was approved.

When the war ended and the town's fighting men returned home, they decided that they didn't like the new name. In 1921, they again petitioned the post office to change the name back to Hermleigh. Washington agreed, and it has been Hermleigh since.

CALLING ALL FINKS — A total of 17 authentic Finks gather at a general store on the Texas-Oklahoma border each year on the third Saturday in June.

In underworld slang, a "fink" is one who informs the police on his criminal colleagues. But not a single stool-pigeon has ever showed up.

Fink is a one-store community on the Red River not far from Denison, Grayson County. It started National Fink Day to get publicity for nearby Lake Texoma and annually invites anybody with the surname Fink to come and join the festivities.

REDMEN'S TOWN — Dallas is the unofficial Indian capital of the state.

Since 1957, more than 10,000 Indians representing more than 80 tribes have pitched their permanent teepees in Big D. So says the Bureau of Indian Affairs.

CITY OF DISASTER — It's a wonder that San Antonio ever lasted long enough to become a city.

In 1815, the little hamlet almost was depopulated following political upheavals in Mexico. Three years later, the San Antonio River flooded and destroyed most of the buildings. Indian raids constantly took a heavy toll in lives and property.

In 1834, the population had reached about 2,000 when a cholera epidemic reduced it by half. Two years later, Santa Anna destroyed the Alamo and its defenders. In 1842, the town was invaded and plundered by the Mexicans.

No other city in Texas has faced such disasters as San Antonio has, and managed to survive.

NAMED LATE — San Augustine rightfully claims to be the second oldest town in Texas (Ysleta is older), but it didn't get its present name until 1807.

When "the cradle of Texas" was first settled, it was known as Tequitina. It was renamed San Augustine when Antonio Leal went there to take possession of lands which had been claimed and occupied many years before.

STARS AND STRIPES TOWN — The only Texas town to be named for the American flag was settled by German immigrants.

It is Old Glory, in eastern Stonewall County. Settled in 1903, it was called New Brandenburg originally. During World War I, however, anti-German sentiment was so prevalent that the citizens decided to show their allegiance to the U.S. in a very practical way. They gave their town the nickname of the flag.

TOWN THAT WILL NOT DIE — For many years now, Old Zapata on the Rio Grande has been dead. It died in the summer of 1954 when Falcon Dam backed up the waters of the river and covered what had been a town of 1,700 people.

The people moved to a new site and built another town. But Old Zapata refuses to die. When the waters of Falcon Lake recede seasonally, the old bridge, part of the highway and sometimes the top of the old courthouse rise out of the water — a ghost town that still returns to haunt the new Zapata.

POST OFFICE IN CHURCH — Mission, in the Rio Grande Valley, was named because the nearby Lomita Mission served as its post office for many years.

Originally, the community was called Conway after an early developer. When it was given a post office in 1908, however, the name was changed to Mission. La Lomita, "the little hill" mission, was restored in 1937 and still stands on the outskirts of the city.

DINOSAUR CAPITAL — Somervell County, in North Central Texas, has the only courthouse in the state graced by the statue of a dinosaur — and with good reason.

The Paluxy River, which flows through the county, was mostly mud 135 million years ago. Dinosaurs abounded in the area and many left their tracks in the mud which now is the limestone bed of the river. As a result, Glen Rose, the county seat, is the unofficial "dinosaur capital" of the U.S.

The dinosaur tracks, which still may be seen along the Paluxy, have become a tourist magnet.

TEMPTATION'S TOWN — In 1869, Dallas was such an evil place that Texas Presbyterians decided against locating their new Westminster College there.

Dallas, which had 2,000 souls in residence at the time, lost out to tiny Tehuacana, in Limestone County. The church leaders picked that hamlet because "it was free from the temptation to vice abounding in various towns."

Westminster later became Trinity, was relocated in Waxahachie in Ellis County and then moved to San Antonio in the 1940's.

TIME MARCHES ON — When Caldwell County built its new courthouse at Lockhart in 1893-94, it made no provision for amenities such as rest rooms. They would have been useless anyway since the town had no sewer system.

A few years later, however, Lockhart installed a modern water plant and sewers. The county commissioners followed suit and ordered the courthouse broom closets turned into proper facilities for men and women. The new plumbing wasn't the final answer to the problem, though.

Weldon Hart of Austin, Texas' leading courthouse historian, says that the first month's water bill was so high after the toilets were installed that the county judge padlocked the rest rooms to reduce expenses!

BUT NO HOT WATER? — At least one Texas home boasted the luxury of an indoor bathroom in frontier days.

Enoch Jones, who built a two-story stone home at Von Ormy, Bexar County, in 1854 included what is believed to be the first complete indoor plumbing system to be installed in a private house in Texas. The house is still in use as a residence.

LILLIE WAS WRONGED — Lillie Langtry, the English actress who achieved world fame in the 1880's, died believing that a Texas town was named for her. It wasn't.

Judge Roy Bean, the famed "Law West of the Pecos" and long-time Val Verde County peace justice, started the legend because he was fascinated by Miss Langtry. She had come originally from the Isle of Jersey and billed herself as "The Jersey Lily." Bean named his combination store, pool hall and courtroom at Langtry in her honor, but the sign painter couldn't spell and it came out "The Jersey Lilly."

Bean never met Miss Langtry but he wrote her many long letters which she never answered. She finally acknowledged one in which he told her that he had named the town of Langtry for her.

Langtry actually was named for a construction foreman who built what is now the Southern Pacific Railroad. It got its name long before Bean moved there and made it famous.

DOUBLE MEANING — Dublin, Erath County, used to be known as Double In.

When Indians frequently attacked the earliest settlement there, the residents would yell, "Double in!" This was the signal for several families to gather in the houses that seemed easiest to defend. Later the term became the community name.

HOLLYWOOD BY THE ALAMO — San Antonio gets the credit for producing the first motion picture ever to win the coveted "Oscar" of the Academy of Motion Picture Arts and Sciences.

The film was "Wings," the classic story of World War I fighter pilots. Starring Clara Bow, Charles "Buddy" Rogers and Richard Arlen, "Wings" was filmed in 1926 at Fort Sam Houston, Kelly Field and other military installations around San Antonio.

Filming took place during the fall of 1926 and "Wings" was released early in 1927. It became one of the all-time hit pictures of the silent screen.

LOVE HAS MANY FACES — When the Ellis County courthouse was being built at Waxahachie in the 1890's, the stone mason on the job fell in love with Miss Myrtle Frame, the beautiful telegraph operator at the railroad station.

As a result, he preserved Miss Frame's face for posterity. The mason carved it into columns at almost every entrance to the building.

SAUNA, DALLAS-STYLE — When the Dallas suburb of Oak Cliff got its water from deep artesian wells, it flowed through home faucets at a temperature of more than 110 degrees.

This was fine for fanciers of hot baths, but a problem for those who liked their water cold. Many residents would draw their tub 12 hours in advance so the water could cool before they bathed.

Then a drought hit in the 1950's and the wells were closed. They haven't been used since.

UNITED WE STAND — One of the first Civil War memorials erected in Texas honors the Union cause, not that of the Confederacy. It still stands today in the Kendall County town of Comfort.

The monument honors a group of Union Loyalists from Gillespie, Kendall, Kerr, Edwards and Kimble Counties who, while en route to Mexico under Major Fritz Tegener, were attacked by Col. James Duff's Confederates. The battle, which occurred not far from Fort Clark in Kinney County on August 10, 1862, killed 27 of Tegener's men. Eight others surrendered and were shot later.

For three years, the bodies of the Texas Unionists lay unburied. In 1865, a group of Comfort residents brought the bones to that community, buried them in a mass grave and erected the memorial on August 10, 1866.

WHISKEY'S TOWN — A bottle of whiskey helped to make Marshall the capital of Harrison County.

When the voters decided to move the county seat from Pulaski, landowners vied to have it built on their property. One Peter Whetstone, himself a member of the locating commission, especially wanted the new courthouse built on his 160 acres. The others visited the site, but decided that it was too dry.

Whetstone then played his trump card. He pulled a large black bottle from a nearby hollow tree and passed it around. Each commissioner took a long swig, then agreed to take another look at the property. They decided that Whetstone's 160 acres weren't dry at all and directed that the new town be laid out on the site.

WELCOME, TRAVELER — In 1911, a San Antonio bawdy house operator published a directory of the sporting district. Object: To make things easier for the visitor looking for a night on the town.

The so-called "Blue Book" was sold by hack drivers. It not only listed the names and addresses of the ladies of the evening, but rated them A, B and C.

MIRACLE WATER — The almost miraculous cure of a mentally-ill woman gave Texas one of its best-known resorts.

The woman, her husband and several children stopped one March day in 1878 in a valley near where the Brazos comes winding out of the Palo Pinto Hills. Because the woman was obviously very nervous and often "out of her head," the husband decided to stay in the valley awhile.

The family built a cabin and the husband dug a well. The water had an unusual taste, but they all drank it. And very soon, the wife recovered.

Word of the strange cure of the demented woman drifted back east to Dallas, and soon another family with a mentally-ill wife moved to the settlement. Soon she recovered also, and the story of the "Crazy Woman Well" spread.

A town sprang up on the site and was named Mineral Wells. And the water — still known as Crazy — attracts health-seekers from everywhere.

GOLFERS NOTE — Galveston had the first golf course and country club in the state. It was opened to members in 1848.

WHAT'S IN A NAME? — Some Leon County citizens have gone from poor to wealthy without changing their jobs or social status.

The community where they live was called Poor when it was established in the 1880's. Later the name was changed to Wealthy.

OLDEST TOWN — Although Ysleta, El Paso County, claims to be Texas' oldest town, Old Tascosa, in Oldham County, actually is the oldest settlement that is still inhabited.

Fred V. Studer, an Amarillo archaeologist, has discovered ruins of an Indian pueblo built on the present site of Old Tascosa about 900 A.D. That's the basis for Tascosa's claim of being Texas' oldest.

Ysleta, settled in 1682, might be called the only "naturalized" town in Texas. It was located in Mexico when it was founded. Later the Rio Grande River changed its course and "gave" Ysleta to Texas.

FIRST NAMED — Anaqua, in southern Victoria County, was the first town in Texas to have a name.

Discovered by Cabeza de Vaca, it already was peopled by Anaqua Indians. By 1820, it boasted a ranch and a chapel. It had become a sizeable town by 1905 when the Missouri Pacific built its line five miles to the east and the settlers began to drift away.

NOTE TO DRINKERS — Denison, in Grayson County, boasts what may be the only public monument in Texas erected in honor of a saloon-keeper.

The monument (in a parkway of the 700 block of Woodard Street) honors Justin Raynal, a pioneer bartender who left his estate to the city for the purpose of buying a site and erecting a school building. Today the Raynal School is still a part of the Denison public education system.

TOWN NOBODY SEES — Near U.S. Highway 83, 18 miles southeast of Perrytown, in Ochiltree County, is one of the state's least heralded tourist attractions. It is "The Buried City" that once was home to the Pueblo Indians.

Discovered by archaeologists in 1907, the ruins include more than 1,000 rooms. Only about 70 of these have been excavated, however, and may be seen by visitors.

HE LIKED IT — When the railroad agreed to build across Jonathan Pierce's Matagorda County ranch in the 1880's, the old rancher was so pleased that he decided to christen his private station "Thank God."

The railroad objected, however, and finally Pierce agreed to call the station "Blessing" instead. That's its name today.

TOWN THAT WOULDN'T SELL — In 1920, Walter D. Cline, then mayor of the oil boom town of Wichita Falls, offered to buy the entire town from the taxpayers. They wouldn't sell.

It all came about when the citizens voted a bond issue for parks, water and sewage works, then discovered that there wasn't enough collateral in the form of tax revenues to redeem them. Mayor Cline solved the problem by notifying property owners that their tax rates had just been doubled.

When the taxpayers balked at the higher assessments, Cline and a friend offered to buy everybody's property. This show of confidence in the future of Wichita Falls so impressed the citizenry that they accepted the 100 per cent tax increase without further protest.

FRANCE IN TEXAS — There is no need for Texans to cross the Atlantic to enjoy that French touch.

Both Castroville and D'Hanis, on Highway 90 in Medina County, were settled in 1849 by 2,000 French immigrants whose descendants remember their Gallic heritage. French and Alsatian are still spoken around Castroville's European-style square, and its more-than-a-century old St. Louis Church has its prototype in dozens of country villages throughout France.

THE WEATHER DID IT — Dew, in Freestone County, was known as Sunshine for more than 20 years. For some reason, the postal authorities decided that the name had to be changed, and the residents swapped Sunshine for Dew.

BELIEVE IT OR NOT — The Dallas post office once was in Nacogdoches, almost 200 miles away. And Denison's first country club was hundreds of miles away at Creede, Colo.!

Dallas depended on the Nacogdoches post office for mail during the days of the Republic of Texas when Nacogdoches County covered half of East Texas, including what is now Dallas County.

Denison located its first Rod and Gun Club in Colorado because the members preferred fishing and hunting to golf. Nobody objected to making the long trek west because they always stayed at least two weeks.

TOWN WITHOUT A NAME — Some sort of citation for a perverse sense of humor goes to an unknown Post Office Department official for naming Texas towns.

In 1879, settlers in a northwestern Travis County community requested a name for their village. They submitted six names, but all were turned down.

"So let the post office be nameless and be damned," one irate settler told Washington. And that's how the village officially became Nameless — and remained so until the post office was closed in 1890.

COMMUNISTS IN DALLAS — Dallas was the site of the only large-scale experiment in communistic living ever attempted in Texas.

In April, 1854, Prosper Victor Considerant, a French socialist, established a colony called La Reunion only four miles from the present Dallas County Courthouse. The land was owned jointly, but every colonist was assigned a portion to cultivate. After the crops were gathered and sold and all bills paid, the profits remaining were distributed equally among heads of families.

Meals were served in a communal dining hall where the prices were based on the age and sex of the diner rather than the amount eaten. This and some other rules eventually caused dissension, and the colony was disbanded in 1867.

ODD TEXAS — Houston is the only city in the world with a stock exchange where no stock is traded.

Chartered in 1933 by Attorney Charles E. Heidingsfelder, Jr., the Houston Stock Exchange has no trading floor and no share of stock has ever been bought or sold through it. It is listed in the Houston telephone directory, but rarely receives any calls.

About the only time there is any activity around the Houston Stock Exchange is once each year when Heidingsfelder and the two other stockholders in the operation get together and hold an annual meeting

IT COULD BE WORSE — Saspamco, in Wilson County, claims the unique distinction of being Texas' only town named for a sewer pipe company.

In 1910, the San Antonio Sewer Pipe Manufacturing Co. began using the red clay in the area for the manufacture of its products. A community sprang up, and took its name from the company initials.

MOST OF THE LEAST — Loving County, in far West Texas, has neither a bank, a railroad, a doctor, a hospital nor a major highway, yet it may be the richest county in the U.S.

Only 226 people live on its 647 square miles, yet its tax valuation is in excess of $6 million. It hasn't recorded a birth in more than 35 years, and it may be the nation's only county without a cemetery. (Its only reported death in recent years was in a traffic accident.)

Loving County was created by the Legislature in 1887, but it had no formal county government until 1931 when a county seat was established at Mentone — its only town.

FOR IKE AND SAM — Shrines honoring two of the nation's most famous political leaders — one a Democrat, the other a Republican — are located only 28 miles apart. Hard by the Red River and Lake Texoma at Denison, on U.S. Highway 75, is the gabled, two-story white house where President Eisenhower was born. Half an hour east, on U.S. 82, is the Georgian marble library honoring the late Sam Rayburn, "Mr. Democrat" to two generations of Americans. Near the library, on the outskirts of Bonham, is the colonial plantation house that was home to Mr. Rayburn.

TEXAS BRAG — Corsicana may be the only city in Texas where every high school graduate is virtually assured of a college education if he wants it. Since 1924, citizens of Corsicana have spent almost $130,000 sending worthy students to college. This year, 75 Corsicana students are attending college on scholarships ranging from $100 to $800.

DRAMA ON BUFFALO BAYOU — On June 11, 1838, the first professional theatrical performance ever given in the Republic of Texas was presented in a Houston hall.

The play was a comedy called "The Hunchback" and President Sam Houston, who was on hand for the performance, described the leading lady as being "as pretty as a head of swamp cabbage."

After the show, her husband took an overdose of laudanum to quiet his nerves and died. Houston placed the Executive Mansion at her disposal and local gamblers made up a purse of gold to help assuage her grief.

THE TOWN THAT MIGRATED — Booker, in northwestern Lipscomb County, is the only town that ever moved itself bodily from another state to Texas.

In 1919, the town of La Kemp, Okla., decided to locate on the railroad when the Panhandle and Santa Fe Railway extended its line from Shattuck, Okla., to Spearman, Tex. The site its citizens picked was across the line in Texas.

The town moved everything from Oklahoma to Texas, including the post office. It took its new name of Booker from a Santa Fe engineer who laid out the line.

CHINATOWN — San Antonio, which has the largest Mexican population of any Texas city, also has more Chinese. The city's 2,500 Chinese operate 15 restaurants, 85 grocery stores and uncounted laundries.

BIG G — Galveston, with a population of 13,818, was Texas' largest city in 1870. San Antonio was second with 12,256. Houston and Dallas were hamlets.

"SHOW ME" STATE IN TEXAS — Marshall, in Harrison County, once was the capital of the State of Missouri.

In 1861, Governor Claiborne F. Jackson of Missouri, a Confederate sympathizer, became fearful that Union troops might invade his borderline state. To escape such an invasion, he moved the Missouri government first to Jefferson, Tex., and then on 19 miles west to Marshall. Here a group of other Missouri Confederates already had established a colony.

The Missouri government was headquartered in Marshall until Lee surrendered and the Confederacy collapsed.

INSECTS NAMED IT — Bug Tussle, in Fannin County, got its name because two early settlers couldn't agree on what to call the community. They were arguing heatedly about the matter one day when their attention was distracted by a couple of tumbling bugs.

"Look at those bugs tussle," one remarked — and the town was named.

FIRST SCHOOL TAX — Galveston was the first Texas city to collect a tax for the purpose of establishing and maintaining public schools.

On April 2, 1846, the Texas Legislature passed a law permitting Galveston to levy a tax not to exceed one-half of one per-cent of the value of real estate within the town limits for the benefit of its schools.

PARADOX — Best, in Reagan County, was known as "the town with the best name and the worst reputation" between 1929 and 1932 when it was the center of the Big Lake oil boom.

SHIP SHAPE — Algoa, Galveston County, may be the only town in Texas named for a ship.

During the 1900 hurricane, a British ship named the *Algoa* was driven ashore ·and remained there for 16 months. When a community sprang up on the site, it was named for the ship.

NOTE TO SCHOLARS — Denison, in Grayson County, had the first free graded school in the state.

HISTORY'S TOWN — Every street in Point Comfort, Calhoun County, is named either for a president of the Republic of Texas, a governor, a hero or a historic site.

PILLAR OF SALT? — The only monument to salt in the state stands on the courthouse square in Palestine, Anderson County.

The granite marker is a reminder of the importance the Confederacy once attached to this household staple. Actually, the Palestine Salt Works was located 6.5 miles southwest of the town during the Civil War and the government controlled the price of the salt produced at $8 per 100-pound sack.

This was considered a bargain since private customers, when they could find salt for sale, paid $20 for 100 pounds.

TEXAS' FIRST SCHOOL — The state's first real public school was taught in the Villa of San Fernando de Bexar (San Antonio) in 1746.

DULL LIFE IN KEENE — In Keene, a Johnson County community southwest of Dallas, the grocery stores sell neither meat nor cigarettes and the U.S. post office closes on Friday afternoon and Saturday, but is open all day Sunday!

Keene is a town of Seventh-Day Adventists, a sect which doesn't eat meat, use lipstick, smoke, drink or dance. It observes Saturday as the Sabbath and regards Sunday as the first working day of the week.

NO ELVES IN FAIRY — Fairy, in Hamilton County, is hardly the land of the leprechauns. It was named for Miss Fairy Fort, daughter of a Confederate Army captain.

THEY COMPROMISED — When postal authorities wouldn't let the residents of a Collin County town name their community "All Together," they compromised and called it Altoga.

BOOM TOWN — Since 1836, when it was founded, the population of Houston has doubled every 11 years!

GOOD CENTS! — When a Hunt County community was denied Money, it took Cash instead. And it's still called Cash today.

Citizens tried to name their town for J. A. Money, the first postmaster, but Washington rejected that name in favor of Cash.

KNUTE'S TOWN — Texas has only one community named after a football coach and he was a native of Sweden who never got any closer to his namesake town than Austin, 40 miles away.

The town is Rockne, Bastrop County, and it honors the immortal Knute who once coached the Fighting Irish of Notre Dame.

WHAT'S IN A NAME? — Legend has it that the Falls County town of Stranger (pop. 27) got its name because a visiting postal official stopped a pedestrian and asked him to suggest a name for the post office.

"I shouldn't," was the reply. "I'm a stranger here."

So Stranger became the town name.

WHAT'S IN A NAME? — When settlers arrived in Kendall County, near the confluence of the Guadalupe River and Sister Creek, the setting was so beautiful that they decided that anybody living there would fare well.

They named their community Welfare.

Beef Barons and
Trail Hands

WHEN THE COWBOYS STRUCK — Texas cowboys called their first and last strike in 1883.

A group of riders working for Panhandle ranches that year organized the Cowboys' Association and served notice on their employers that they would quit if their wages weren't upped from $30 to $50 a month. They also demanded $50 monthly for the chuck wagon cook and $75 for the ramrod, or boss.

Although more than 300 cowboys were involved, the strike failed. The cowpunchers established their headquarters near the rip-roaring old frontier town of Tascosa and promptly spent their money in the dance halls and gambling dives. In a few days, their money gone, they went back to work.

HOW IT BEGAN — Ranching was an established and flourishing business in Texas long before the first Anglo settlers arrived.

The "father" of the cattle business in what is now Texas was Alonso de Leon, a native of Cadereyta, Mexico. Between 1686 and 1690, when Spanish authorities feared French encroachments from the north, he made five attempts to explore and colonize Texas.

On his last expedition in 1690, he founded the mission of San Francisco de los Tejas in East Texas. He stocked it with horses and cattle. He also turned loose cattle at every river crossing, and these turned to the wilds and continued to increase in number.

A year later, the King of Spain sent Don Domingo Teran de los Rios to become Governor of the province of the Tejas Indians

(Texas) at an annual salary of 2,500 pesos. To help feed himself and his contingent of soldiers, the new governor brought along herds of cattle and horses. He also distributed some of the cattle he brought to the missions east of the Trinity River.

Thus ranching already was a way of life when American colonists arrived 125 years later. Not only did the missions run cattle herds, but ranching had spread from the missions to individuals. It was a ready-made business for the new settlers.

WHEN LONGHORNS WERE GAME — Texas Longhorns, now an honored breed of cattle, once were so despised by ranchers that they were hunted down and killed like buffalo.

Once Texas ranchers began importing Herefords and other fine beef cattle, they had little use for the Longhorn. When the Circle Dot Ranch was closed out in the 1890's, some of its rangy old Longhorns escaped to the Glass Mountains north of Marathon in the Big Bend. Later they began to come down from the hills and lead the ranch-bred Herefords back to their lair.

In 1900, one rancher — E. E. Townsend of the Elsinore Cattle Company — decided to end the depredations of the Longhorns. Armed with a Colt .45, he rode into the mountains, chased down every Longhorn he could find and killed it on the spot.

ON THE TRAIL — Few ranchers had either the money or the manpower to conduct the great cattle drives from Texas to northern railheads. As a result, most of the cattle went to market under the watchful eye of a specialist known as a trailing contractor.

Even after the railroads came to Texas in the 1870's, few ranchers could afford to ship their cattle to market by rail. The railroads charged from $5 to $5.50 per head for the service — far more than it cost to walk the beef to market overland.

The trailing contractors charged a flat fee of only $1 or $1.25 a head. For this they furnished a trail boss, drovers, wagons and all supplies. Because they could handle thousands of cattle in a single drive, they could still turn a good profit.

One of the largest of the trail contractors herded an estimated 500,000 head of cattle from Texas to Dodge City, Kansas, between 1876 and 1887.

BURIAL BALLAD — One of America's immortal folksongs was inspired by the tragic death of a young drover whose grave may still be seen today in a Wilbarger County cotton field.

The cowboy's name has been lost to history, but he was with a drive herding Longhorns up the trail in 1885. While camped at

Doan's Crossing, near the present city of Vernon, he accidentally shot himself and died.

Next morning, the other drovers buried him in a lonely grave a mile from Doan's Store and the drive moved on. Two cowboys named Pink Burdette and Jesse James Benton were much moved by the death, however, and they made up a song in memory of the young drover. They called it "Oh, Bury Me Not on the Lone Prairie" and it has become an American classic.

ONE FOR THE ARMY — A cowboy or a cavalryman: which was the better horseman?

To find out, a U.S. Army major and a top rodeo rider once raced their mounts more than 300 miles through Central Texas.

On January 13, 1922, Major Terry Allen, mounted on a stallion that was part thoroughbred and part quarter horse, rode away from Dallas' Adolphus Hotel. At the same time, Key Dunne of Sierra Blanca, one of the best rodeo riders on the circuit, left Fort Worth riding a famous Mustang named A.W.O.L.

The route was via Waco, Temple, Austin and San Marcos to San Antonio's Alamo, with the race to end on the fifth day. Major Allen covered the 301.1-mile course seven hours and 34 minutes ahead of Dunne. He thus proved (to the Army, at least) that the cavalry was better than cowpunching in the development of horsemanship.

BUT NO BEADS YET? — Old-time cowboys would turn over in their graves if they knew that more and more cattle are wearing earrings these days instead of a brand on their hides.

Branding with a hot iron damages the hide so that it often is useless for making leather goods. As a result, ranchers are giving up the time-honored brand and identifying their cows by painting them, putting rings in their ears or using dry ice to freeze a brand in place.

ONE TURN OF PITCH AND TOSS — Texas Rickard, the uneducated cowboy from Clay County who went on to become president of New York's Madison Square Garden, was a born gambler.

Once, while operating an elaborate gambling house in Dawson, Alaska, during the gold rush, Rickard bet his prosperous house of chance on one draw for high card — and lost. Undaunted, he got a job chopping wood at $15 a cord, built himself a new stake and died a millionaire.

He also had a public service career that few boxing fans ever heard about. In 1900, while prospecting in Alaska, he was elected mayor of Nome — the first and only Texan ever so honored.

IT TAKES ALL KINDS — "The Cowboy," one of the best sculptures of its kind in existence, stands today on the Capitol grounds in Austin. Strangely enough, it was done by a woman from New York who knew little of the West and was living in Paris at the time.

Madame Constance Whitney Warren did her lifesize cowboy in her studio in Paris. She placed him, sombrero in hand, astride a bucking pony. She displayed the statue in Paris but intended to give it to an American state.

Largely through the efforts of Charles Cason of Houston and Gov. Pat M. Neff, "The Cowboy" was obtained for Texas in 1925.

PAINTER ON HORSEBACK — Frank Reaugh was never a cowboy on a working ranch, but he is the painter who is credited with immortalizing the Texas Longhorn.

Born in Illinois in 1860, he came to Texas with his parents in a covered wagon in 1876 and settled on a farm near Terrell, Kaufman County. There he began to sketch livestock on the nearby open range. Thus began a career that was to earn him the title "dean of Texas artists."

His master work, a series called "24 Hours with the Herd," was given to The University of Texas at Austin. The Panhandle-Plains Museum in Canyon owns more than 500 of his pastels. Other large Reaugh collections are owned by the Dallas Public Library and the Dallas Historical Society.

Reaugh spent the last 55 years of his life in Dallas. After his death in 1945, his studio became the home of the city's Creative Arts Center.

IT WON'T HOLD WATER — There is no such thing as a 10-gallon hat. Or a five-gallon one, either, for that matter.

The fact that ranchmen describe the size of their headgear in gallons has no relation to the amount of liquid the crown of the hat will hold. Actually, they're using the Spanish word, "galon" — and it's spelled with only one l. It's the name of the decorative braid (often in gold or silver) that Spanish vaqueros have worn on the brims of their sombreros for centuries.

A 5-galon hat means that it has five rows of galons or braid around the brim and a 10-galon hat has ten rows. Some even have 15.

THE TRAIL NOBODY KNOWS — Texas' least known and least used frontier highway was the Chihuahua Trail.

It was made in 1839 when some 200 residents of Chihuahua, Mexico, decided to open trade with the U.S. by breaking a new, shorter trail. The trail crossed the Rio Grande near where Presidio now stands, passed near the present towns of Alpine, Fort Stockton and Snyder, continued on by the sites of Sherman, Bonham and Paris and on north across the Red River.

In 1840, the trail-blazers returned to Mexico. After that, the trail was never used as a trading route again.

SADDLE COPS — Computers are putting the cowboy back in the saddle — the stolen saddle, that is.

Now when a rider loses a saddle, he reports the theft to the Texas and Southwestern Cattle Raisers Association instead of the sheriff. He answers 18 simple descriptive questions about the property and the answers go into a computer. When the Fort Worth organization spots a saddle that appears to be stolen, they check with the computer. If the description fits, an arrest follows.

DRUG STORE COWBOYS? — Old-time cowpokes may have been good ranch hands, but they wouldn't have dared compete as bronc riders in a modern rodeo.

Most of them were what ranchers called good "straight riders" — men who could make a saddle horse perform all sorts of range chores. Only a few, however, had much experience riding the ornery bucking horses that are the stars of today's rodeos.

FROM CIRCUS TO RANGE — A circus that visited Houston in the 1890's inadvertently gave Texas a new breed of cattle.

Among the spectators that day was Shanghai Pierce, whose ranching interests spread from the Colorado River to the Gulf. He was attracted by one of the acts that used a couple of sacred cows from India, and finally decided to buy them and have them shipped to his Rancho Grande.

He found that these thick-skinned animals were particularly adapted to the humid Gulf weather. Later, his nephew, A. P. Borden, continued to experiment with the Indian cattle and eventually developed today's Brahma breed.

BEEF BARONS — Old-time ranchers were a democratic lot, but they had much in common with Europe's feudal lords.

Their ranch often was larger than many European countries. The ranch house, like the feudal castle, was the seat of all authority. Their cattle brands were guarded as carefully as any princeling's coat of arms.

Perhaps their cowpunchers didn't don armor to fight for a cause. But roping contests and rodeos aren't far removed from the knightly tournaments of old.

WHEN KNIGHTHOOD WAS IN TEXAS — Surely the descendants of old King Arthur himself must have ridden the open range a hundred years ago.

In those pre-rodeo days, Texas cowboys enjoyed a riding contest in which the riders called themselves "Knights of Chivalry" and bedecked themselves with ribbons before mounting their steeds. Armed only with a seven-foot spear, their object was to impale five small rings suspended from five poles along a 300-yard course.

The contestant who could pick up all five rings with his spear while riding at full tilt had the privilege of naming the "Queen of the Tournament."

THE NEGRO COWBOY — In the myth and legend that has grown up around the Old West, the impression is that all cowboys were tall, lean, tanned — but white. They weren't.

Some historians estimate that there were more than 5,000 Negroes among the cowboys who went up the cattle trails in the years following the Civil War. Col. Charles Goodnight, Oliver Loving and many other Texas ranchers regularly employed Negro riders on their trail drives. Many were trail bosses and several became successful ranchers.

BUTLER FOR BULLS — Rocking Chair Ranch, Limited, which once sprawled over some 250 square miles of the Panhandle counties of Wheeler and Collingsworth, provided a staff of "servants" for its 14,000 cattle.

The ranch's British owners insisted on calling their range riders "cow servants" since their job was to look after the cattle. And the cowhands, angry at this affront to their noble occupation, derisively nicknamed the spread "The Nobility Ranch" — a name which old-timers still use when they refer to it.

THEY HAD THE HABIT — Line riders on the old XIT Ranch must have set some kind of a record for smoking.

In 1891, a Dallas merchant received from the ranch an order for a freight car load of cigarette papers!

TELEGRAPHIC LULLABY — Cowboys didn't sing on the range to put the cattle to sleep. Actually songs were used by the night herders to keep in touch with each other in the dark, to drown out any strange noises that might stampede the cattle and to help a man keep himself awake in the saddle.

Cowboy ballads weren't the only songs drovers sang to keep cattle calm on the trail. They often sang hymns and what was called "opera" or "opery" songs.

The "opera" songs had little kinship to grand opera, however. They were the hit tunes turned out by the professional song writers of the time. Two of the favorites heard by thousands of cows on hundreds of cattle drives were "Silver Threads among the Gold" and "After the Ball is Over."

THE COWBOY IS A DUDE — Westchester County, New York, was the first "range" of the cowboy. The word "cowboy" originally was given Tory marauders who harassed American patriots of Westchester during the Revolution.

TEXAS TALK — Much of the dialect of Texans, particularly those in the cattle business, is anglicized from Spanish.

Lariat, for example, comes from *la reata*, meaning to tie back or rope. Brasada, the Texan's word for brush country, is from the Mexican word *brazada*, which has the same meaning. Chaps, the leather breeches worn by cowboys, is a short version of three Spanish words — *chaparreros*, *chaparreras* or *chaparajos*.

Some Spanish words have come into the Texas dialect unchanged. Corral, meaning yard or enclosure, is one.

A .45 WAS BIG MONEY — Because there was a scarcity of small coins in circulation in the early days, Texas cattlemen used different sizes of six-gun cartridges for quarters and dimes. They called it "cowboy change."

NO HIGHWAY SIGNS? — There were no markings to guide the drovers who punched cows over the great cattle trails.

Trails were natural driveways as much as 40 miles wide and often more than 1,000 miles long.

WHY COWHANDS GET GRAY — When George W. Littlefield started a new ranch in 1877 near Tascosa, he decided that his cattle brand would be the letters LIT.

This wasn't an unusual brand, but applying it to the cows was quite a job. Major Littlefield insisted that the L be on the left shoulder, the I on the side and the T on the hip of the animal. Three separate branding irons were required.

FOR ONE CENT, TOO — Leather post cards used to be common in Texas. The "cards" were about the size of today's contemporary greetings, but were made of leather. Some were sold with messages printed on them; others had spaces where messages could be written in ink. They went out of use, largely because of rising costs, before World War I.

HOW IT BEGAN — Driving cattle up the trail to markets was the brainchild of a cowboy and a businessman.

One day in 1867, J. J. Myers, a Texas cow-hunter and one-time member of the Fremont Expedition, and Joseph H. McCoy, an Illinois businessman, met at Junction City, Kans., where the Santa Fe Railroad tracks stopped. While sitting on a stack of lumber, they decided that money could be made if Myers would gather cattle in Texas, drive them overland to Kansas railheads and let McCoy ship them on to eastern markets.

The idea wasn't new. A few herds already had been driven up the trail. But once Myers and McCoy got their plan working, trail driving became big business and cattle raising became Texas' biggest industry.

FIRST RODEO? — The first official record of a rodeo was an informal gathering of the top hands from several ranches at Pecos, Reeves County, in 1883. Just for the fun of it, the cowboys got together to determine which brand boasted the saltiest ropers and riders.

Later in the 1880's, bronc riding and steer roping were among the festivities at a cowboy reunion staged in the Panhandle town of Tascosa. Then, in 1888, the first contest rodeo with prizes was staged at Canadian, Hemphill County, and a new sport had come to Texas to stay.

TRAVELING TEXAS — Tourists who have a yen to travel over an old cattle trail need only to get on a modern Texas expressway.

Several highways follow the old trail routes closely. One expressway (Interstate 35) follows the Old Chisholm Trail almost exactly for several miles between Salado and Belton, in Bell County.

WHAT'S IN A NAME? — Samuel A. Maverick, whose name today is applied to any unbranded cattle, was not a rancher himself and never owned but one herd of cows.

He was an attorney and real estate speculator who, in 1845, took title to 400 cattle in settlement of a debt. He turned the herd over to a Negro family in his employ who simply let the cattle graze, fatten, multiply and wander away.

Neighbors who were quick to brand their own cattle recognized the unbranded cows as belonging to the Maverick herd. They began calling all unbranded calves "mavericks" and thus gave the language a new term.

Folklore That Is Fact

LOVE STORY — The continuing love of a sculptor for his dead sweetheart gave Texas and the world one of its art masterpieces — the "Rose Window" of San Antonio's San Jose Mission.

The sculptor was Pedro Huisar, who came to Texas from Spain in the 1700's. His dream was to establish himself and then send for his childhood sweetheart, his Rosita, or "little Rose." He found work at the mission and soon wrote Rosita to come to the New World.

En route to America, however, her ship sank and all lives were lost. Huisar, his heart broken and his plans for the future shattered, began carving a window at the mission in memory of his beloved Rosita.

It took him five years to complete the window with its intricately carved scrolls that remind one of blooming roses. And when the job was done, Huisar never cut another stone.

LONE STAR LEGENDS — Timothy O'Hara and his Irish tenor voice, so some say, gave the word "gringo" to the Texas vernacular.

'Tis said that O'Hara, who supposedly lived in the area around San Antonio, knew a song called "Green Grow the Lilacs," which he sang constantly. One day some friends from a distance came to visit him and they inquired of a Mexican how to find Mr. O'Hara.

"O'Hara?" the Mexican asked. "I know no one by that name. But Senor Greengrow, the singer, lives down the trail."

From then on, everybody called O'Hara "greengrow." This was corrupted to "gringo" by the Mexicans, and soon became their name for any American.

LIGHTS OUT — The old story about the farmer who tried to blow out the first gas light he ever saw really happened in Fort

Worth and with tragic consequences.

On November 28, 1876, Quanah Parker, the famed Comanche Indian chief, and his friend, Yellow Bear, checked into a hotel there which had just installed artificial gas lights. The Indians thought the lamps were the kerosene variety and blew them out when they went to bed. The gas fumes killed Yellow Bear and Chief Parker barely escaped with his life.

LEGENDS THAT LIE — It isn't true that the Texas jackrabbit can outrun a race horse, but he won't be left at the gate.

While a good nag can run about 34 miles an hour for a mile or so, the jackrabbit has been clocked at only 28 miles per hour. But leaping ten feet at a time and more than 200 leaps a minute, he has been known to hit 45 miles an hour on the straightaway.

AND TELL OF TIME — Few early Texans knew what time it was on cloudy days. Clocks and watches were rare and most settlers depended on home-made sundials to keep time. These were made by setting three stakes a few feet apart and in line with the North Star. When the shadows of these stakes formed a straight line at the spring or fall equinox, it was exactly 12 noon.

Next a line was drawn perpendicular to the south end of this first line, extending in both directions. From the point of intersection, a semi-circle was drawn on the north side of the line and marked with the numbers on a clock face.

When the sun was shining brightly, the dial was a fairly accurate way of telling time.

GOOD DEED KILLED TOWN — Because the kindly citizens of a Texas river town ministered to a dying wayfarer, they sounded the death knell for the biggest port ever located along the Trinity.

The town was Cincinnati, founded in 1838 in the northeastern corner of Walker County. Within 15 years, the town was a bustling business center of more than 600 people. Its wharves were regular stops for whole fleets of riverboats.

Then one night in 1853, a traveler en route from Palestine to Galveston arrived at Hunter's Tavern with a raging fever. Mrs. Hunter put him to bed and nursed him for two days. Feeling a little stronger, he boarded a boat but died before it reached Galveston.

Not long after, Mrs. Hunter became ill. The disease spread by the stranger was yellow fever, and within weeks, half the population of Cincinnati died of it. Those who survived tried to keep the town going, but river traffic began to wane and Cincinnati never recovered. Today a cemetery plot is all that remains.

RARELY TOLD TALE — After World War I, when quicksilver was discovered in the Big Bend, a New Yorker came to Terlingua hoping to pick up a bonanza from some unwitting rancher.

At the first ranch he visited, he found no quicksilver and almost no grass. However, it did have acres of maguey — or century plant — which he mistook for a new kind of giant asparagus. The rancher assured him that this was the only place in the world that produced 12-foot stalks of asparagus, but that Texans wouldn't eat the stuff.

The New Yorker, visualizing a vast new market for "Texas-size" asparagus among Eastern gourmets, bought the ranch on the spot.

WHERE GOBLINS ROAM — A drive down the famous Ghost Road in the Hardin County piney woods can be a memorable experience.

For more than half a century, residents of the Big Thicket have spotted a weird red light bouncing along the dirt road that runs straight as an arrow from the old ghost town of Bragg to Saratoga. Although seen often, the light has always managed to outdistance pursuers.

Legend has it that the light is that of a lantern carried by a switchman killed near Bragg many decades ago when that town was served by the Santa Fe Railroad.

WHAT'S OUR NAME? — Residents of this state have been known in print as Texans, Texians, Texonians, Texasians, Texicans, Texanos, Tejanos and a half dozen other descriptive terms.

Today "Texan" probably is the word most used to identify a citizen of the Lone Star State, although "Texian" still crops up in print. The late J. Frank Dobie was among those who insisted that "Texian" was the only correct word.

It certainly was one of the earliest used. R. Henderson Shuffler, director of the Institute of Texan Cultures in San Antonio, says that "Texian" was invented by an editorial writer on the New Orleans *Bee* in 1835. The writer decided that it was time that somebody picked one word for general use.

Quoted in "Riding Line," newsletter of the Texas Historical Association, Historian Shuffler says that "Texian" was generally used in referring to citizens of the Republic of Texas. Once Texas became a state, the "i" was dropped and we have been "Texans" since.

NO JUICY FRUIT? — The habit of chewing gum is as old as that of smoking in Texas.

Early settlers discovered that the hardened sap of cypress and cedar trees provided an acceptable chew — if one didn't mind the turpentine flavor and certain adhesive qualities. Later, the sap of the sweet gum tree proved to be even more palatable, particularly when a mint leaf was added for flavor.

It remained for some unknown and unsung experimenter, however, to produce a kind of frontier delicacy. By adding the elastic-like meat from a type of brier berry to a wad of sweet gum, the result was a product which enabled the practiced user to produce blue-colored bubbles!

TEXAS-SIZED CHEW — The capture of the Mexican general, Santa Anna, at the battle of San Jacinto may have given chewing gum to the world.

After the battle, Santa Anna was imprisoned for a while in New York and he took with him a wad of chicle from Yucatan. When he was freed, he left the chicle behind and it came into the possession of a man named Adams.

Adams was intrigued with the chicle and decided to experiment with it. Eventually he discovered that it was good to chew when processed correctly and flavored. Thus was born the chewing gum industry.

LEGENDARY TEXAS — Many hundreds of moons ago, the dying wish of a Caddo Indian chief brought about the founding of one of Texas' oldest cities.

The chief had two sons. One, Natchitoches, was black-haired and swarthy. The other, Nacogdoches, was blonde and blue-eyed. As he lay dying, the old chief commanded his sons to split the tribe.

Natchitoches was to gather his wives and children, turn his face toward the rising sun and, after three days of travel, stop and build a new home for his tribe. Nacogdoches was to do likewise, but he was to take his people toward the setting sun.

Thus were the twin tribes of Natchitoches and Nacogdoches founded exactly 100 miles apart. Nacogdoches became the father of the Tejas, the Indians of East Texas. And today the towns of Natchitoches, Louisiana, and Nacogdoches, Texas, stand where the old Indian villages once stood.

STRANGE BUT TRUE

OPIATE OF THE MASSES — Texas' only annual religious ceremony in which the law permits hard narcotics to be used by the worshippers takes place at Mirando City, Webb County.

Members of the Native American Church, a Christian sect to which about 300,000 Indians belong, eat peyote buttons, the beans of the mescal cactus, as a sacrament. The dreams induced by the drugs are said to promote contemplation among the members.

Because peyote is regarded as a sacrament by the New American Church, members are granted a special immunity from Federal narcotic laws.

MONUMENT TO A STAR-GAZER — An East Texas banker who preferred looking at the stars to lending money is responsible for the world's third largest telescope being located in the Lone Star State.

He was William J. McDonald, who was born in Paris in 1844. A self-educated lawyer, he turned to finance and founded banks in the northeast Texas towns of Paris, Cooper and Clarksville. His first love, however, was science and especially astronomy. His principal hobby was observing the stars through a small telescope.

When he died in 1926, he left an estate of almost $1 million to The University of Texas "to erect and equip" an astronomical observatory for the promotion and study of the science of astronomy. Today the McDonald Observatory, atop Mount Locke near Fort Davis in West Texas, is one of the largest and best installations of its kind.

MONUMENT TO A CAVE MAN — Alley Oop, the

leading character in a comic strip about cave men, is honored with a statue in the Pecos County town of Iraan. In fact, Iraan may be said to be the home of Alley Oop and the stone age world he inhabits.

V. T. Hamlin, the artist who created the unique comic strip, lived in Iraan for many years and used to prowl the Pecos River to uncover relics of the cave people who once populated the area. He used these experiences as the basis for the story of Alley Oop.

THE COMFORTS OF HOME — Wharton County's jail

has a telephone jack in each cell!

They're not there for the convenience of prisoners, however, and no telephone instrument is ever plugged in just for a social call.

A former county sheriff, T. W. (Buckshot) Lane, had the telephone jack installed after a prisoner used a call from his lawyer as a ruse to attempt an escape. As sheriff Lane (who rarely wore arms) was escorting the prisoner from his cell to the jail office to receive the phone call, the prisoner pulled a smuggled gun.

Lane and jail guards subdued him, but the sheriff ordered the phone jacks installed shortly after. Now when a prisoner's lawyer calls, the telephone is carried to the cell.

AND TELL OF TIME — After an absence of many years,

Napoleon's clock again is ticking away in the Governor's Mansion in Austin.

The clock, built for the French Emperor about 1805, was discovered in a New Orleans antique shop by Miss Ima Hogg, daughter of Governor James Stephen Hogg. She purchased it for Mrs. Cleveland Sewall of Houston and Mrs. Sewall gave the clock to the Mansion in 1943. It fell into disrepair and was stored in the basement.

A few years ago, Mrs. Allan Shivers, wife of the former governor, told the then first lady, Mrs. Preston Smith, that Napoleon's old clock was stored somewhere in the Mansion. Mrs. Smith found it, had it restored by inmates of the Texas Prison System and today it is one of the top tourist attractions in the Mansion. It is valued at between $80,000 and $100,000.

PHYSICIAN, WATCH THYSELF — Indian herb doc-

tors aren't exactly posing a threat to their modern counterparts, but they are talking about organizing the Original American Medical Association.

R. Henderson Shuffler, director of San Antonio's Institute of Texan Cultures, says that medicine men from the various tribes may soon establish an exchange of information on herbs and "prescriptions."

74

Idea for the organization originated when W. W. (Bill) Keeler, chairman of the board of Phillips Petroleum and also principal chief of the Cherokees, visited the Institute of Texan Cultures. There he met Rocky Stallings, a Tonkawa tribesman who works in the Indian exhibits and is an expert on native medicinal herbs. Now they're planning a round-up of other tribal medicine men.

THE CHANGING TIMES — In the early years of the Supreme Court of Texas, there were no funds with which to employ a court reporter. As a result, lawyers had to find out about court opinions by reading them in the newspapers.

HONEY OF A TOWN — Houston's million-plus citizens still keep an estimated 5,000 beehives, mostly to produce honey for their own tables.

CENTER STAGE — Ulysses S. Grant might have become an actor instead of President of the United States except for an unhappy experience in Corpus Christi in 1846.

Second Lt. Grant was in Corpus with General Zachary Taylor's troops, sent down to Texas because of a boundary dispute between the U.S. and Mexico. The soldiers, bored with inactivity and the lack of recreational facilities in the frontier port, whiled away the time by building an Army Theater.

The theater opened on January 8, 1846, with a play, a short farce, and some song-and-dance acts. Later the soldiers decided to stage Shakespeare's *Othello* and, lacking an actress, drafted Lt. Grant for the feminine role of Desdemona.

All went well until rehearsal. The male lead protested playing romantic scenes with Grant and a professional actress was summoned from New Orleans to replace him. The incident cured any desire Grant may have had to follow acting as a career.

IT'S A FACT — It costs Texas as much to keep its governor in style as it costs the British Empire to keep up Queen Elizabeth and her royal household.

The British queen has to struggle along on an annuity of 475,000 pounds ($1,140,000) to pay the functionaries who serve her at Buckingham Palace. It costs Texas taxpayers about the same to pay its governor and the salaries of his staff for a year.

FIREBUGS ARE WELCOME — The Red River County Bar Association has minutes recording an offer to defend without charge any person who may be indicted for arson after successfully burning the county's courthouse.

The citizens of Clarksville and the rest of the county, however, want to keep the old courthouse. A few years ago, the voters nixed a proposal to replace it with a new one.

County employees don't share the same enthusiasm for the building. To get to his office, one of them has to crawl through the attic, open a trap door and climb down a ladder to get to work.

THERE WERE GIANTS IN THOSE DAYS — Was the area south of Fort Worth once populated by a race of people more than 16 feet tall? Some scientists think so.

Near Glen Rose, in Sovervell County, archaeologists found one skeleton of a woman more than seven feet tall. And along the nearby Paluxy River, other scientists have found footprints more than 21 inches long which appear to be those of human feet. The footprints, first discovered more than 50 years ago, started scientists on a search for the big Texans that is still going on.

The area around Glen Rose has been famous for years as the spot where more dinosaur tracks have been found than anywhere else in the United States. But whether there were giants in those days as well as dinosaurs is a question which science has not yet answered conclusively.

WHAT'S IN A NAME? — The pecan, official state tree of Texas, was given its name by Indians before the white man came to America.

The word "pecan" literally means "bone" — because the Indians decided that the shell of the native variety was as hard as a bone. The pecan is, in fact, a member of the hickory family.

Thomas Jefferson was an early fancier of the nut and planted pecan trees at Monticello. He gave some to George Washington who is said to have carried some in his pocket forever after, munching them as between meal snacks.

FORGOTTEN HEROES — Although little mention is made of it in history books, three Texans of Mexican ancestry were among the signers of the Texas Declaration of Independence.

They were Franco Ruiz, J. Antonio Navarro and Lorenzo de Zavala.

MODERN CHRISTMAS STORY — A salesman, hunting in vain for a parking space on Longview's shopper-clogged streets, tried a fragment of prayer as a last resort.

Leaving his car in a no-parking zone, he stuck this note on the windshield: "I've circled this block ten times and I have an appointment that I must keep or lose my job. Forgive us our trespasses."

A policeman spotted the illegally parked car and note and left this reply along with a summons: "I've circled this block 20 years. If I don't give you a ticket, I lose my job. Lead us not into temptation."

LOST AND FOUND — Texas' most treasured document — its Declaration of Independence from Mexico — was "lost" for more than 60 years.

After its adoption March 2, 1836, at Washington-on-the-Brazos, it was taken to Washington, D.C., by William H. Wharton. He filed it in the Department of State on May 28, 1836.

For the next six decades, the document was all but forgotten in the State Department archives. Finally, 60 years, three months and one day after its adoption, the Declaration of Independence was returned to Texas — on June 3, 1896. It now is on public display in the Texas State Library in Austin.

CAPITOL NEVER COMPLETED — Texas' red granite capitol, largest state house in the U.S., has never been completed!

Elijah E. Meyers, the Detroit architect who planned the building, designed each of the side entrances with two-story porticoes which were never added.

Even without the side porticoes, it was the seventh largest building in the world when it was opened in 1888. It remains one of the three buildings in the world to have a double dome. The others are St. Paul's Cathedral in London and the Vatican (St. Peter's) in Rome.

TEXAS FIRST — On September 6, 1830, the *Texas Gazette* published the first murder story to appear in a Texas paper when it reported a slaying in San Felipe de Austin.

DOES TEXAS OWN ITS CAPITOL? — It's possible that the State of Texas does not have true title to the land on which the Capitol is located.

The Capitol and other state buildings, as well as a part of The University of Texas, are located on about 1,500 acres of land in Austin originally patented to one Samuel Goucher. The Goucher tract was part of a much larger site selected by five commissioners appointed by the Congress of the Republic of Texas in an act passed on January 14, 1839.

Most of the land had been patented originally to General Thomas Jefferson Chambers before the Revolution, but he had failed to perfect his title with the new Republic after the War of Independence. By the time he got around to filing for his title in 1840, the Bastrop County Land Office (Travis County had not been created), ignorant of Chambers' claim, had made a number of new grants out of land which Chambers apparently owned. The Goucher tract, granted on March 2, 1838, was one.

Later General Chambers went to court to protect his claim. It was finally settled in 1925 when the Legislature paid $20,000 to his surviving daughters, Mrs. Katie Sturgis and Mrs. Stella MacDonald of Galveston. This seemingly cleared the state's title except for the Goucher tract.

In 1838, most of the Goucher family had been killed in an Indian raid and the land passed to other claimants. Years later, however, three of the Goucher children reappeared with a story of having only been kidnapped by the Indians. One of them sold his interest in the family land, but neither of the surviving daughters or their descendants ever conveyed their interests.

Thus some legal authorities believe that there is a question still as to whether or not Texas actually owns the land on which its capitol stands!

HISTORY'S HOAX — For years, one of the standard reference works on the fall of the Alamo was a book called *Col. Crockett's Exploits and Adventures in Texas.*

Supposedly it was the diary which old Davy kept almost until the moment he died at the Alamo. The publishers swore that a Mexican soldier had found it on Crockett's body.

It became a best seller as soon as it was published in 1837 and several European editions were printed. When sales began to dwindle after a time, the publishers admitted that it wasn't Davy's diary after all. Realizing the sensational value of Crockett's martyrdom at the Alamo, they had hired a commercial hack to write the fictitious "diary" before the smoke of battle had cleared away.

HISTORY ON THE WALL — Some of the reports of the proceedings of the General Council of the provisional government of Texas were preserved for posterity on green wallpaper!

Paper was in short supply when the government convened at San Felipe de Austin and regular foolscap was soon exhausted in recording committee reports and ordinances. The wallpaper was used while a new supply of regular paper was being ordered from a dealer in Columbia.

BLUE NORTHER — It can get cold in Texas. At Tulia, Swisher County, the mercury dropped to 23 degrees below zero on February 12, 1899 — the lowest temperature ever recorded in the state.

JUDGE BEAN; BOXING PROMOTER — The only world's championship boxing match ever staged in Texas was a box office failure but a bonanza at the bar.

It was held in 1895 on a sandbar in the Rio Grande across from Langtry. The promoter was Judge Roy Bean, the "Law West of the Pecos," and the principals were Bob Fitzsimmons and Peter Maher, then champion of Ireland.

Boxing was illegal in both Texas and Mexico, but Bean promised the promoters "protection" if they would hold the bout in mid-river and give him the beer concession. They agreed.

Fewer than 400 paying fans came — not enough to pay expenses. However, they bought almost a freight carload of Bean's beer at $1 a bottle, giving his Jersey Lily Saloon the most successful day in its history.

And the fight? It wasn't much. Fitzsimmons took only a minute and a half to knock out Maher. Then the fans went back to enjoy more of Judge Bean's beer.

THE ALAMO'S SECOND COMMANDER — Most history books ignore it, but the fact is there were two different men who commanded the defense of the Alamo.

Colonel William Barret Travis, the senior officer of the Texas defenders, was killed before the Alamo fell. Captain John J. Baugh, a Virginian, then succeeded to the command. By the time he was killed a few hours later, there was no need to elect a new leader. The Alamo had fallen.

HOW ABOUT FOOTBALL, TOO? — Going to prison is one way to get into a fraternity or sorority in Texas.

Alpha chapter of Chi Alpha accepts as pledges only those who are inmates at Wynne Prison Farm outside of Huntsville. For the girls, there's the Beta chapter at Goree Farm. And like all good fraternities, Chi Alpha expanded recently with a Gamma chapter at Eastham Prison Farm near Weldon.

Like their counterparts in the collegiate world, the prison fraternities and sororities have strict membership requirements and the initiation rituals are secret. They even have a "faculty advisor" — the prison chaplain!

MURDER UNDER THE DOME — Guides rarely mention it to tourists but the State Capitol once was the scene of a murder.

State Comptroller R. M. Love was chatting with a former employee one day in 1903 when the visitor pulled out a gun and shot him. An assistant grabbed the gunman and the pistol discharged a second time, dropping the assassin.

The gun-wielder died in the first floor corridor, and Love died later the same day.

AND TELL OF TIME — San Antonio's Ursuline Academy and Convent has a tower clock with four faces — but only three dials.

Legend has it that when the clock was built in 1868, nobody lived on the north side of town and probably never would. Since there would be nobody on the north who had need of the time of day, the dial on that face was left off.

NOT FOR SALE — At the Joseph Men's Shop in Austin (where President Johnson bought his size 7 headgear for years), there are two Stetsons which are not for sale.

One is a wide-brim, low crown "Open Road" — the kind of Texas hat that LBJ preferred. The other is the "Sierra" model which women like to wear when they dress in western clothes. Both hats were ordered by Governor John Connally as gifts, and they were to have been delivered to him the afternoon of November 22, 1963. They never were.

Etched in gold script on the inside band of the "Sierra" are the initials "JBK". In the other, "JFK". They were to have been gifts to President and Mrs. Kennedy at a $100 a plate dinner scheduled for that evening in Austin. The President was assassinated a few hours earlier in Dallas and Governor Connally was gravely wounded.

DID YOU KNOW? — Those red, white and blue mail boxes originated in Texas.

A few years ago, San Antonio Postmaster Dan Quill, tiring of the drab green that was the official postal color, ordered a few letter drops repainted as an experiment. Washington liked the idea so well that it ordered all U.S. mail boxes and mail trucks into the paint shop.

FRONTIER PHARMACOPOEIA — Dentists were rare in early Texas, but home remedies for toothache were common.

One home médical book said that the pain could always be halted by picking the offending tooth with a coffin nail, a splinter from a tree struck by lightning, the middle toe of an owl or a needle used in making a shroud.

INDIAN STOMP — Those dances staged for tourists at the Alabama-Coushatta Reservation near Livingston aren't traditional to this tribe.

In the old days, these East Texas Indians could dance with the best of them. Then the missionaries came and the tribes were taught that dancing was sinful. It became a lost art.

A few years ago, when tribal leaders decided to open their reservation to tourists, they had to call in members of other Indian tribes to teach them their dances.

QUICK, THE SMELLING SALTS — Camphor, that aromatic spirit once so prized by ladies who were prone to fainting spells, still grows in Texas.

Wharton County has the only known camphor trees in the state. They were planted in 1907 on a farm near Mackay because the U.S. Government then used camphor in making gunpowder and hoped Texas' climate would provide a steady source. The trees grew, but the government found another ingredient that it preferred for its munitions and Texas camphor was never produced for sale.

FIRST TRANSPORTATION TAX? — Taxes paid by passengers arriving at the port of Galveston financed the first public hospital in the Republic of Texas.

The Texas Congress approved the hospital on August 31, 1845, but specified that it was to be built by assessing passengers on all incoming boats at these rates: 50 cents for adults, 25 cents for those under 16 and 25 cents for each passenger traveling in steerage.

TEXAS BRAG — The French Embassy in Austin is the only such building ever erected by a foreign power in the United States outside of Washington.

RARELY TOLD TALE — A Texas television station holds some kind of record for long-distance and long-lasting transmission.

In September, 1953, television screens in many parts of England suddenly began projecting the identification card and call letters of Station KLEE in Houston. It was such a unique phenomenon that some viewers took photographs of the image.

But that's only half the story. Station KLEE went off the air in 1950 — three years before its signal was picked up in England!

PAINTINGS DOUBLE AS PHOTOGRAPHS — Two of the most accurate works of art ever produced in Texas hang in the Senate chamber of the capitol at Austin.

They are Harry Arthur McArdle's paintings, "Dawn at the Alamo" and "The Battle of San Jacinto."

To make sure that he would picture the scenes correctly, the artist interviewed Mexican soldiers who had participated in the battle of the Alamo and survivors of the battle of San Jacinto. These included Santa Anna himself.

BIBLIOPHILES, PLEASE NOTE — The first book ever written about Texas was a best seller. It was La Relacion, Cabeza de Vaca's story of his explorations in what is now the Lone Star State. It was first published in Spain in 1542, but was so popular that a second edition had to be run off 13 years later.

No copy of the first edition is known to exist. The few copies of the second edition sell for $10,000 and up.

HOMEMADE FUNERALS — Professional undertakers aren't needed under Texas law — if a relative wants to handle the last rites for a loved one.

A body doesn't have to be embalmed if it is buried within 24 hours. A blood relative may prepare the body at home, build the coffin himself and transport the corpse to the cemetery in his own vehicle (after getting burial and transportation permits from health authorities).

Unless the cemetery objects, the relative also can dig the grave. He also can have any kind of services he wishes, or none at all. He can bury the body, too, if he complies with state law and cemetery regulations.

GOOFY GEOGRAPHY — There is one place where Louisiana is WEST of Texas.

Among the marshes and canals along the Sabine River channel off the coast of Orange, there is an island that is claimed by Louisiana, although it is west of another island belonging to Texas.

BUT NO TEXAS ARMY? — Texas, the only State in the Union with the right to maintain its own navy, has its own air force, too. And, it's the only one of its kind in the world.

It's the Confederate Air Force headquartered at Rebel Field in the Rio Grande Valley town of Mercedes. The C.A.F. has only one mission — to maintain a museum of the great fighter planes used by all sides in World War II. Its ultimate goal is to have a complete line of the fighters in flying condition and ready to go.

BARBERS WERE SCARCE, TOO — Texas once had more blacksmiths than it had preachers, and farmers outnumbered ranchers by almost 25 to 1.

The 1860 census listed 1,290 blacksmiths in the state and only 758 clergymen. There were 51,569 farmers and 2,576 ranchers and stockmen. Physicians were plentiful, with 1,471 listed as practicing.

Most Texans must have cut their own hair a century ago because only 41 barbers were listed in the entire state. Eight citizens gave their occupation as architect, but there were only two who were listed as bankers.

WORLD'S LARGEST BOOT CAMP — No other state had such a wide range of military activity as did Texas in World War

II. It is estimated that 1,250,000 men, representing all branches of the service, trained here.

IT'S THE LAW — There is an old Texas law, ignored for years, which requires locomotives to display a Lone Star flag at all times.

PRISONERS FOR HIRE — It used to be that anybody willing to bid enough could rent his own private labor force from the state penitentiary.

The Legislature, having no money with which to operate the prison, hit on leasing as an answer to the problem. From 1868 until 1883, lessees could take complete charge and furnish everything needed for the welfare of the prisoners and the upkeep of the system. In exchange, the lessee could work the convicts at any kind of hard labor.

In 1871, Ward, Dewey & Company leased the entire Huntsville Prison from the state with the right to "sell" the services of 927 inmates. Their largest customers were the railroad builders who rented convicts to lay rail.

It was a profitable arrangement for everybody except the prisoners. The state was paid $5,000 annually for the first five years of the contract, $10,000 annually for the next five and $20,000 annually during the last five years of the 15-year lease.

COLBERT'S FERRY — A ferry started by a chief of the Choctaw Indians served as a major transportation link between Texas and Oklahoma for well over half a century.

The chieftain was B. F. Colbert, who moved to the Indian Territory from Mississippi in 1846. Settling on the Red River, he acquired a 500-acre plantation, steam sawmill, grist mill and cotton gin. In 1853, he established his ferry at a site just north of the present Texas city of Denison.

Later he built a $40,000 wagon bridge across the Red River at that point. His 577-foot wooden bridge (16 feet in width except for a center section 24 feet wide to permit wagons to pass) was one of the first toll spans across the river.

FIRST QUIZ SHOW — For better or for worse, the first quiz show originated in the Lone Star State.

More than 40 years ago, a young announcer named Parks Johnson began interviewing passersby in front of Houston's Rice Hotel for Station KTRH. One night it was cold and rainy and there were no pedestrians around to be interviewed. To get them on the street, Johnson offered a dollar bill to anyone who would come out and answer questions on "Vox Pop."

Within minutes, a crowd was on hand and a new national craze was born. Johnson took "Vox Pop" to New York where it became the first of the big network quiz shows.

STRANGE LEGACY — When Ed Singleton was hanged in Beeville back in 1877, he willed his skin to the district attorney who convicted him.

He directed that the skin be made into a drumhead and that it be beaten to the tune of "Old Molly Hare" in front of the Bee County Courthouse on each anniversary of his hanging.

NO MORE HANGINGS — Texas' last public hanging took place in Waco on July 30, 1923. Hanged was Roy Mitchell, confessed killer of eight. More than 5,000 Waco citizens, including an estimated 500 women, turned out to see Mitchell die.

THERE'S ONE IN PENNSYLVANIA, TOO — One can visit East Texas without ever crossing the boundaries of the Lone Star State.

East Texas is a community in Lehigh County, Pa.

TEXAS OKIES — It's possible to have been born in Texas, never to have moved from one's birthplace and yet to have lived in Oklahoma for more than seven decades.

This would be true of anyone who happened to have been born in Mangum, Greer County, Tex., before 1896. In that year, the U.S. Supreme Court took Greer County away from Texas and gave it to the Indian Territory. Ten years later, when the Territory became the State of Oklahoma, portions of Greer County formed two new counties and part of another.

Part of Texas' original "Lost County" remained intact, however, with Mangum as the county seat — but still in Oklahoma.

IN TECHNICOLOR, TOO — Flying saucers (and orange ones, at that) have been flitting through Texas skies for almost a century.

Credit for giving the name "saucer" to these unidentified flying objects belongs to a Grayson County farmer named John Martin. Martin sighted such an object while hunting one day. And on January 25, 1878, he described it to the Denison *Daily News* as an orange colored disk that "resembled a large saucer."

BIG HITTER — Baseball just isn't what it used to be.

In a game between Corsicana and Texarkana on June 15, 1902, a Corsicana catcher named Justin (Nig) Clarke set some kind of a

Texas League record by hitting eight home runs in eight times at bat.

In fact, there was little joy in Texarkana that night. Corsicana clobbered the visitors by a score of 51 to 3.

The Business of Texas

"THE DEVIL'S NECKLACE" — John W. (Bet-a-Million) Gates, then a brash young hardware drummer, introduced barbed wire to Texas ranchers in 1877 with a feat of salesmanship that has rarely been equaled.

Gates erected a barbed wire fence on San Antonio's Military Plaza and filled it with 50 rough and tough Longhorn steers. Then he bet the assembled ranchers $100 against $10 that the fencing which is "lighter than air, stronger than whiskey and cheaper than dirt" would hold the steers against anything.

To prove it, Gates hired a rider carrying a flaming torch to whip the herd into a stampede. The frightened steers lunged into the fence, snapping a mesquite post, but the wire held. This demonstration convinced the ranchers, and barbed wire had come to Texas to stay.

HOW IT BEGAN — It was a German immigrant rather than a Mexican who brought chili to Texas and the U.S.

In 1892, William Gebhardt opened a restaurant in the back of a New Braunfels saloon and began serving up old country delicacies like sauerbraten. He soon discovered, however, that Texans — even German immigrants — liked chili.

It was strictly a seasonal food, however, because chili peppers were available only when they could be grown in home gardens. In order to serve his customers every month of the year, Gebhardt began importing ancho chili peppers from Mexico.

Then Gebhardt conceived the idea of developing a product that would permit housewives to prepare chili the year around. After months of experimenting by grinding up chili peppers, he came up with a powder that could be packaged and kept indefinitely. With the new chili powder, a whole new food industry was born in Texas and the U.S.

POLITICAL BOSS — William Madison McDonald, the son of ex-slaves and the first Negro ever to be president of a Texas bank, also wielded considerable power in the state's politics from 1896 to 1912.

For four decades, McDonald headed the Fraternal Bank & Trust Co. of Fort Worth. A protege of Col. E. H. R. Green of Dallas (the son of Mrs. Hetty Green, the colorful and erratic financier), McDonald developed close ties with the Republican Party. For many years, he was the most powerful Republican in the state.

To his friends, McDonald was known as "Gooseneck" — a nickname given him because he was tall and slim and had an unusually long neck. He was 86 when he died in Fort Worth in 1952.

TEXAS FIRST — America's first streamlined train with rubber tires began operations on a Texas railroad.

The Texas & Pacific Railway purchased the two-car, gasoline-powered streamliner in 1932 for use over its "Transcontinental" branch between Texarkana and Dallas. The experimental train wasn't successful and didn't continue in service, but many ideas embodied in its construction were used in later streamliners.

SUCCESS STORY — In 1910, a farmer named Tom Huston was looking for a way to market the peanuts he grew near Henderson, Rusk County.

He began packaging the shelled and roasted nuts in a package that bore a picture of a peanut attired in a top hat, monocle, spats and a cane. The idea sent customers flocking to buy the product and packaged peanuts have been an international favorite since.

MISSING MINERAL — No really important gold deposit has ever been found in Texas.

For awhile, a small amount was mined at the old Heath mine northeast of Llano in Llano County. Some gold has been produced as a by-product by the silver mines around Shafter, in Presidio County. Traces of the mineral have been found in many parts of the state, but never in quantities large enough to start even a mild gold rush.

ROUTE OF THE APOSTLES — The old Bartlett and Western Railway (abandoned many years ago) had four stations named Matthew, Mark, Luke and John.

In each station was a framed copy of the gospel written by the apostle of that name.

LEGENDS THAT LIVE — One winter more than 100 years ago, an itinerant peddler came through the area south of Houston selling what he said were small magnolia trees.

Unsuspecting buyers wondered at their strange appearance, but planted them anyway. The next spring the trees bore fruit — a new variety of fig never seen in the area. It was named, appropriately, "Magnolia."

Today the Magnolia fig — which refuses to grow anywhere except in an area along, and 50 miles inland from, the upper Gulf coast — is a major industry. Each year about 400 acres of the prize figs are grown in a 20-mile radius of the Galveston County town of Friendswood.

HISTORY OF CANVAS — Traveling salesmen in early Texas often were looking for a farmer's daughter — but only to paint her picture.

Portrait painting was in vogue about the time the Republic of Texas was established. Many an itinerant peddler, taking advantage of this desire of rural customers to leave their likeness to posterity, added paints and canvas to their pack and became painters of people.

Calling themselves "limners," these roving artists usually asked $10 (a very high price in those days) for a portrait. Many a proud parent paid the fee willingly, and today some of these primitive paintings are collector's items.

THE PASSING PARADE — The Dallas Cotton Exchange trading room, which once could boast that more of this commodity was traded there than at any other place in the U.S., no longer welcomes buyers and sellers. It is leased to a computing company.

Trading in cotton still goes on, but now it is conducted in one small room of the 16-story Cotton Exchange Building. The Dallas Cotton Exchange, built in 1926, once was the largest building in the world devoted to a single commodity. Today half the space is leased to other forms of business.

WHAT'S IN A NAME? — A popular Texas-made cigar got its name because it was made originally for the exclusive enjoyment of the members of a San Antonio club.

In 1910, H. W. Finck, who had been manufacturing cigars in San Antonio since 1893, joined with other socially prominent citizens in establishing the Travis Club. It was a multi-storied downtown club where prominent Texans gathered to eat, drink and enjoy good cigars. Women, of course, were barred.

For members only, Finck made up a special "Travis Club"

cigar. But during World War I, when the club patriotically opened its doors to servicemen, outsiders also got a chance to sample the special cigars. When the war ended, former soldiers continued to order "Travis Club" cigars — and the brand still is a best-seller today.

TONGUE FOOLERY — An early-day Houston lawyer-banker had the unique name of Decimus et Ultimus Barziza.

It seems that Phillip Ignatius Barziza had gone to one of the numerous taverns in Williamsburg, Va., to celebrate the birth of his tenth child. He confided to a friend that he had used up all of the fine old family names (he was a descendant of an Italian nobleman) and didn't know what to christen his latest.

"Barziza," the friend advised, "name him Decimus et Ultimus (Latin for tenth and last) and make it so."

In 1875, "Tenth and Last" Barziza became the first president of the Houston Land & Trust Co. (now Houston Bank and Trust). He also was Houston's most noted criminal lawyer of his time.

BAD GUESS? — Texas' great store, Neiman-Marcus, may have been founded on poor business judgment.

Before the famous Dallas-based retail store was opened in 1905, Herbert Marcus, Sr., his sister, Carrie Marcus Neiman, and her husband, Al Neiman, had operated a successful sales promotion business in Atlanta. They decided to put it up for sale.

They had two offers — one for $25,000 in cash and the other an exclusive franchise to market a new soft drink in the state of Missouri. They had some doubts about the success of the new drink, so they took the cash and used it to open the Dallas store.

The drink was Coca Cola.

UNUSUAL UNION — One of the most unusual labor organizations in Texas history was organized in Galveston September 11, 1866, as the Screwmen's Benevolent Association.

Limited to the relatively unskilled trade of those who manipulated screwjacks to pack cotton bales in the holds of ships, the Screwmen's Benevolent Association existed until 1914 when it became a local of the International Longshoremen's Association.

CLEANLINESS PAYS — Employees at a carbon plant in Seagraves, Gaines County, get paid extra for taking a bath!

To be sure that employees go home without being covered with the plant's sooty product, they are furnished with washing machines, soap and soft water in which to launder their clothes. And they're paid time and a half for an extra 30 minutes provided that they use the time to take a shower.

CAPITOL TALE — A chunk of rock that couldn't be traded for a good saddle horse built Texas' big pink granite capitol in Austin.

Robert S. Weddle, writing in *Southwest Heritage,* tells the story of how G. W. Lacy, who owned Granite Mountain near Marble Falls, once tried to trade it for a saddle horse. He got no takers for the huge mass of rock in Burnet County.

In 1881, however, Texas began building a new capitol and Lacy and his partners decided to donate the granite needed. The state gratefully accepted the offer.

Nine years later, Lacy sold Granite Mountain for $90,000. From Lacy's 640-acre mountain that couldn't be traded for one horse has since come millions of tons of granite worth hundreds of thousands of dollars.

BATTER UP — One of the state's most unique museums is housed in a Houston furniture store!

Some years ago, when the Finger Furniture Co. acquired the old Buff Stadium as a site for its new store, the last home plate used on the field was installed in the furniture store at the same spot where it had once served the greats of baseball. With the plate as a starter, Sammy Finger, president of the company, built the Houston Baseball Museum.

Among the hundreds of mementoes, the museum includes what may be the world's largest collection of autographed baseballs. Included are balls autographed by 45 members of the Baseball Hall of Fame as well as three which were tossed out (and later autographed) by U.S. presidents.

OLDEST UNION — Galveston's Local No. 7, Brotherhood of Carpenters and Joiners, was organized in 1860. It is one of the oldest continuously functioning labor organizations in the U.S.

THE UNCHANGING TIMES — To see how banks were run before the days of drive-in windows and pretty girl tellers, drop in at 226 West Commerce Street in San Antonio and visit D. & A. Oppenheimer Bankers (Unincorporated).

The Oppenheimer is one of 21 private banks left in the U.S. — six are in Texas — and it may be the only bank in the nation that has never published a statement of condition. Organized in 1858 at Rusk, it has been a San Antonio institution since shortly after the Civil War.

Its owners have never gone modern, either. The bank is housed in a 100-year-old granite block building with steam radiators, exposed pipes, a linoleum floor and an ancient Mosler "screw door" safe. To lock the safe, an employee rotates the entire threaded door, detaches the handle and then hides it!

TEXANS AT WORK — Because performers in Ringling Brothers' Circus liked fruit cake, a Texas bakery has become internationally famous.

When Corsicana's Collin Street Bakery began baking fruit cake in 1898, almost none of the local townspeople would buy it. Then the circus arrived for a show at the beginning of the Christmas shopping season and performers sampled the new product. They liked it so well that they ordered hundreds of cakes sent to their friends and families throughout the world.

Since then, the orders haven't stopped. Each Christmas, the bakery ships almost a million pounds of fruit cake to every state and 107 foreign countries.

HARD SELL? — Texas has an industry that has been doing business at the same site for more than 12,000 years!

It's the flint quarry on the Alibates Ranch on the banks of the Canadian River north of Amarillo. The Palaeo-Indians dug the quarries during the Ice Age and used the hard flint for weapon points with which to hunt mammoths.

Successive tribes of Panhandle Indians continued to use the quarries. Today the site is a national monument.

SORCERER'S STORE — Laredo's "Casa Tijerina" doesn't sell witches' brew, but it does manufacture a floor cleaner that's guaranteed to keep the broomstick brigade from invading a home.

Texas' only manufacturing pharmacy of faith cures sells everything from dove's blood (for kidney malfunction) to oil of coyote fat (for rheumatism). And for those uninitiated in the powers of healing by sorcery, there are booklets on hypnotism, black magic and palmistry on sale.

Fernando Tijerina, the astonishing apothecary, welcomes all comers at the corner of Gustavus and Tilden Streets in Laredo.

POST EXCHANGE? — Eagle Hardware Store at Eagle Pass can claim that it has outfitted an army.

In 1915, the President of Mexico sent a trainload of soldiers across the Rio Grande to Eagle Pass and told the owners of Eagle Hardware to outfit the troops with horses and saddles. In one week, the border store sold the Mexicans almost 5,000 horses and mules and hundreds of saddles.

OF CHILI AND WOLVES — When a Corsicana company introduced its Wolf brand chili in 1921, it set out to startle Texans into buying the product.

Its salesmen toured the state in Model T Ford roadsters that had been redesigned so that the passenger compartment looked like an oversized can of chili. Riding behind in a steel cage was a real live wolf!

THE GOOD OLD DAYS? — Loan sharks must have had a field day in early Texas.

On March 6, 1848, Anson Jones, last president of the Republic, borrowed $140 from a merchant at Washington-on-the-Brazos. He signed a note agreeing to repay the $140 in 90 days, plus interest of $33.

That's equal to an annual interest of 97 per cent.

IT'S A FACT — Because most Texas real estate laws trace their ancestry to Spain, the Spanish vara, a unit of linear measure equivalent to 33-1/3 inches, is accepted as a legal standard in this state.

COMIC STRIP TOWN — Little Abner isn't a Texan and Texas has no Dogpatch, but the state does have its own version of "Skunk Hollow."

The principal industry of New Harp, in Montague County, is the trapping, raising and selling of skunks and other varmints. Eastern Montague County, which abuts the Red River in North Central Texas, is known as the best "skunk country" in the Southwest. Two varmint-catching businesses operating out of New Harp sell everything from baby armadillos to ring-tails. Buyers are commercial pet shops around the world.

WHEN COAL WAS KING — Many Texans still make a living from coal mining — an industry that employed more than 5,000 people in the state about a half century ago.

Records indicate that the Indians were the first miners, digging lignite for fuel. In the late 1880's, the first bituminous coal mines began operating. By World War I, more than 2 million tons of coal were being taken from Texas mines each year. After the war, the industry slowly declined.

TRAVELING TEXAS — The state's only licensed winery is located on the outskirts of Del Rio in Val Verde County.

In the early 1180's, the Quallia family brought over some grapevines from their native Italy and started the business. It is still a family operation.

WHEN BANKS WERE BANNED — General Sam Houston was so opposed to money-lending that he hoped to keep bankers and banks out of his beloved Texas.

At the Constitutional Convention of 1833, he prevailed on the delegates to insert a clause saying that no bank or banking institution, or office of discount or deposit, or any moneyed corporation or banking establishment, should ever exist under that constitution.

Fortunately, however, the constitution later was amended. When the Congress of the Republic of Texas met for its first regular session at Columbia in 1836, it passed a bill to incorporate The Texas Railway, Navigation and Banking Company. The corporation was never formed, but it paved the way for the state's present banking system.

TEACHING PAYS — Lawrence R. Herkimer of Dallas grosses more than $1 million a year — as a cheerleader!

As head of the Cheerleader Supply Co., Ltd., he conducts up to 85 clinics for high school pep squads each summer in 28 states. He also founded and runs the National Cheerleaders Association, dues $2, and publishes the official magazine, *The Megaphone,* which goes to 10,000 schools and is read by 100,000 students.

Cheerleader Supply Co. also supplies schools with everything from uniforms to pennants and batons to help them keep spirits up.

AUTO GRAPHICS — Col. Edward H. R. Green of Terrell brought the first automobile to Texas in 1899. It was a 2-cylinder "St. Louis" gasoline buggy.

NO POSTCARDS, EITHER? — No postage stamps were ever issued by the Republic of Texas.

The Republic established a postal system in October, 1835, and named John Rice Jones as postmaster general. Rates were set at 6-1/4 cents for a one-page letter traveling no more than 20 miles. The fee was collected in advance by the local postmaster or carrier, and no stamps were used.

PEN MIGHTIER THAN THE SWORD — Printing a newspaper was more important than carrying a gun during the Texas War of Independence.

So in 1835, when a 23-year-old printer from Tennessee named David E. Lawhon arrived in Nacogdoches to enlist in the Texian Army, the recruiter refused to accept him. He told the 6-foot, 4-inch 200-pound editor that Texas needed another newspaper instead of another soldier.

Lawhon accepted the challenge. When his *Texean and Emigrant's Guide* appeared on November 28, 1835, it was a carefully planned piece of propaganda camouflaged as a newspaper. The front page was devoted to English translations of the Mexican laws which Texas was fighting to overthrow.

Like Gail Borden's *Texas Telegraph and Register* (the only other paper of significance published during the revolution), Lawhon's *Guide* also published all of the official ordinances, decrees and resolutions passed by the Texas government.

Lawhon published his paper for only a few months. Having discharged his obligation to freedom, he became a rancher. He died in 1884.

THE BARE FACTS — Modesty may have prevented some of the early settlers in what is now Texas from accepting land grants from the King of Spain. This was because the ceremony in which the land was transferred usually was conducted *au natural*.

When Jose Maria de Balli received his league of what is now Hidalgo County in April, 1768, he was required to appear at the site naked. So did the captain in His Majesty's Royal Army, who was to effect the transfer of the land. The lack of clothing was supposed to symbolize their humility toward God and King.

Standing together nude, the officer read the deed aloud, then took Balli's right hand and walked onto the grant where he formally transferred it in the name of the King. The recipient then picked up some sticks, broke them and flung them into the wind. That was his pledge that he would clear the land in time.

Next he crumbled some of the earth and tossed it into the wind as a symbol that he could plow the soil and live off the land. Only then was he considered to have been given legal possession of the property.

THE GREAT GIVEAWAY — History books ignore it, and the man responsible probably didn't know what he was doing. But the fact remains that Texas, in 1866, perpetrated the biggest giveaway of its resources in its history.

The bonanza was the ownership of all of the ground water, oil, natural gas and minerals in Texas. The man responsible for the giveaway was B. T. Selman, the Smith County delegate to the Constitutional Convention of 1866.

Since 1783, when Spain had reserved title to all minerals, known and unknown, for the king, Texas had retained these rights even on property that had passed into private ownership. When Texas entered the Union in 1845, it retained the right of ownership as a state to all of its minerals.

However, the owners of a small salt lake in Hidalgo County had been issued a private patent by the state in 1847 to sell the salt commercially. During the Civil War, when salt was in short supply, Texas had cancelled the patent and taken control of the output of the lake. After the war, the owners had asked that the patent be renewed.

Selman wanted to see the patent on the salt returned to the owners. To accomplish this, he introduced a resolution at the Constitutional Convention releasing all of the state's mineral rights to the surface owners of the land. On March 22, 1866, the convention approved the ordinance. Texas had effectively given away mineral rights that would be worth as much as $5 billion dollars a year within a century.

BATTLE FOR THE CAMERAS — In 1914, the only war ever waged in order to make a movie was fought along the Texas border.

For $25,000, Pancho Villa, the notorious Mexican bandit general, sold the motion picture rights to the revolution he was fighting. The Mutual Film Corp. sent a special railway car, cameras and a crew to El Paso to follow the action. Villa even agreed that he would fight all of his battles only between 9 a.m. and 4 p.m. — when the light was right for pictures.

He kept his word and coordinated his battles with the movie script. When "The Life of Villa" was released, however, it was a box office failure, and today not even a single print remains of one of the most unusual motion pictures ever made.

JIM BOWIE, RACKETEER — Long before he died a hero at the Alamo, Jim Bowie made a small fortune in the dual role of slave smuggler and stool pigeon.

Jim and two of his brothers would buy illegal slaves from pirate Jean Lafitte on Galveston Island, paying a dollar a pound — about $140 each — for them. Next they would slip them across the line into Louisiana and then inform the customs agents that there were some smuggled Africans abroad in the land.

As required by law, the slaves then would be sold at public auction. The buyers were always Jim Bowie and his brothers. Why? Because the law gave any informer on smuggled slaves half of whatever they brought at public auction.

In this way, the Bowies got legal title to the slaves at half price. Then they promptly took them to Mississippi and sold them for as much as $1,000 a head.

MONEY MAKER — Texas was minting and circulating its own coins long before it became an independent republic.

In the early 19th century, San Antonio merchants found themselves unable to make change because no Spanish coins were in circulation. At the request of the businessmen, the Spanish governor authorized the settlement to mint its own coins in 1814.

Frank W. Brown, present-day San Antonio banker who has researched the subject, says that the first coins actually were made by a jeweler named Manuel Barrera in 1817. The next year, Jose Antonio de la Garza, who was the postmaster, was awarded a monopoly to mint money. He turned out two sizes of copper coins. Known in numismatic circles as "San Antonio money," they are rare collectors' items today.

Facts Not In
The History Books

NOT IN THE SCRIPT — Maurice Barrymore, who delighted in playing tragic roles on the stage, starred in a real-life tragedy on March 19, 1879, in Marshall.

Barrymore had performed in the drama, *Diplomacy*, at the Mahone Opera House and had gone to the railway station with his co-star, Ellen Cummins, to wait for the train. Accompanied by another member of the cast named Porter, they went into the station's Harvey House restaurant for a late supper.

They were sitting at the counter when a man named Currie, passing through the restaurant from the bar, made an insulting remark to Miss Cummins. Barrymore rose from his stool to remonstrate and Currie pulled a gun and shot the famed actor in the arm. Porter leaped up to aid Barrymore and was killed instantly.

Barrymore recovered. Currie was arrested but escaped punishment. And for years after, the theatrical profession regarded Texas as a sort of "no man's land" where sudden death lurked in every bistro.

DAY OF FREEDOM — This June 19, as they have since 1865, thousands of Texans will gather in a Limestone County park to celebrate a holiday unique to the Lone Star State — Emancipation Day.

It was on June 19, 1865, that General Gordon Granger landed at Galveston to assume military rule of Texas and immediately issued an executive order freeing all blacks from slavery. A few days later, a plantation owner named Gouverneur Stroud gathered his slaves together not far from the Comanche crossing of the Navasota River and read the proclamation to them.

Since that day, Negroes have gathered at Comanche Crossing each Juneteenth to celebrate the end of slavery. In 1898, Limestone County blacks acquired 30 acres on the river and dedicated them as a permanent site for the June 19 celebration and homecoming each year.

As many as 30,000 members of the Limestone County 19th of June Association have returned from throughout the U.S. to celebrate Emancipation Day.

WHITE MAN'S PEACE — The only unbroken treaty ever made between whites and Indians in Texas was negotiated by a former German nobleman, John O. Meusebach.

In 1844, Prince Carl of Solms-Braunfels brought a colony of Germans to Texas. The prince had hoped to settle on a grant of land between the Llano and Colorado Rivers which the immigrants had purchased from a couple of sharp promoters named Henry Fisher and Burchard Miller. It turned out, however, that the land was wholly occupied by hostile Indians.

Prince Carl, who lacked both the personality and the business sense to lead the colony, finally got its affairs so muddled that he had to be replaced. Meusebach was dispatched from Germany to get the colony out of debt and settled on the Fisher-Miller grant.

Meusebach made peace with the Indians, settled a new colony at what is now Fredericksburg and then sought out the Comanches in an attempt to get the right to enter their lands. He went into the Indian camp unarmed and won them over with his fearlessness and frankness. On March 2, 1847, he signed a treaty with them. It is the one Indian treaty that was kept by both sides.

SIX FLAGS OVER SAN JACINTO — There were six separate flags flying over the San Jacinto Battleground on April 21, 1836, when General Sam Houston's Army defeated Santa Anna's Mexican Army and won independence for Texas.

One was the green, white and red flag of the Texas Conservatives, and the most popular of the flags used by Texas in 1835 and 1836. Another was the flag of the Texas Liberals, which was a solid blue field with a lone white star in the center. A third flag honored the town of San Felipe.

The fourth was a red bandana which a soldier took from his pocket, tied to a long limb and raised. It was a grim reminder to the Mexicans of how Santa Anna had unfurled a blood red flag at the Alamo, signaling a fight to the death. The bandana symbolized the willingness of the Texans to do likewise.

The fifth banner, known to history as "the San Jacinto flag," had the figure of a woman in the center of a white field. She carried a sword around which was wrapped a banner with the words "Liberty or Death." This flag is preserved today in the House of Representatives at Austin.

The sixth flag, of course, was that of Mexico.

LEGENDS THAT LIVE — Robert L. Ripley, whose "Believe-It-Or-Not" cartoons made him world famous, is said to have conceived the idea for the popular newspaper feature while living in Marlin, Falls County.

Between 1908 and 1924, the New York Giants baseball team traveled to Marlin each March for spring training. One year Ripley supposedly was one of the rookies, but injured an arm and decided to give up baseball for drawing.

One of his first "Believe-It-Or-Not" cartoons concerns Marlin. It tells how Easy Street there leads to education — it runs into the school grounds. And Fortune Street leads to the grave — it's the route to the town cemetery.

CRIME DIDN'T PAY — Legend to the contrary, Sam Bass was a failure as an outlaw.

Crime certainly didn't pay for him — except in notoriety. The only real haul he ever made was the $10,000 he got as a member of the gang that held up a Union Pacific train at Big Spring, Nebraska, in March, 1877. After this success, he organized his own robber band. Their first holdup netted exactly $11.

Sam's gang only grossed $1,000 during the few months that it operated and these robberies were conducted almost entirely without gunplay. In fact, Sam Bass had never shot a man until July 21, 1878, when he decided to rob the bank at Round Rock, in Williamson County. Officers trapped him and he shot his way out, killing a deputy in the process. Sam was shot, too, and died later of his wound.

FIRST YULETIDE — Christmas was first celebrated almost 300 years ago in what is now Texas.

A detachment of soldiers "going to the discovery of the East and the kingdom of Texas" under orders of the King of Spain camped on a hilltop along the Rio Grande near where the town of Presidio now stands. It was Christmas Eve, 1683.

The next morning, Juan Dominguez de Mendoza, commandant of the troops, ordered a special ceremony to celebrate the birth of Christ. It was the first recorded observance of Christmas in Texas.

CORRECTING THE HISTORIANS — Texas, not Massachusetts, was the scene of the first Thanksgiving.

It happened on May 23, 1541, and the site was the Palo Duro Canyon in the Panhandle. Coronado had led his men up from

Mexico looking for a legendary city called Quivera — a place so grand and so rich that the women were said to cook their food in golden pots. The expedition was almost out of food when they stumbled onto the canyon and found a friendly tribe of Tejas Indians living there.

To celebrate his good fortune in finding the Indians, Coronado ordered a day of thanksgiving. Today a plaque erected in Palo Duro in 1959 by the Texas Society of the Daughters of the American Colonists proclaims May 23, 1541, as the "Feast of the First Thanksgiving."

IT TAKES ALL KINDS — Deaf Smith, the scout who destroyed Vince's Bridge before the Battle of San Jacinto, was fond of skunk meat.

Smith was taught by the Indians how to prepare it, and believed that both the scent and the meat had high medicinal value.

SECRETARY'S FRIEND — The first electric typewriter was the invention of the late James F. Smathers, a native of Llano.

In 1914, Smathers patented what was described as the first power-driven typewriter. Nine years later, he assigned his patent to a Rochester, N.Y., company which eventually was purchased by International Business Machines Corporation.

Smathers died in 1967 and was buried in Poughkeepsie, N.Y.

SCHOOL DAZE — Students who dread today's college entrance examinations can be thankful they didn't try to enroll in Rutersville College in the 1840's.

To enter one of Texas' first institutions of higher learning, a student "was expected to know Latin and Greek Grammar, Caesar's Commentaries, Cicero's Select Orations, the Georgics and Aeneid of Virgil, Jacob's Greek Reader or St. John's Gospel in Greek."

There was some consolation, however. Tuition was only $20 and room and board cost only $10 per month.

BIG TEXAS — The longest straight-line distance across Texas is 801 miles.

DID YOU KNOW? — Texas grows 104 species of fruit other than the citrus for which it is famous.

TEXAS FACT — The Lone Star State has 35 million acres of woodland — enough to match all of the famed New England forests except Connecticut.

LONG HOT SUMMER — Seymour, Baylor County, recorded a temperature of 120 degrees on August 12, 1936 — the highest on record in Texas.

HISTORY'S MYSTERIES — Is it possible that what is now Dallas County, Texas, was the original "Garden of Eden"?

Scientists may debate the issue for years, but they are certain of one thing: Charcoal recovered from prehistoric pits near Lewisville have been dated by the latest measuring techniques as being more than 37,000 years old! That's more than twice the age of anything ever recovered from any other archaeological site.

Indications that the area around Lewisville may be the birthplace of world civilization came in the 1950's during excavations for a Trinity River dam. Workers uncovered 21 fire-scarred hearths near the junction of Hickory Creek and the Elm Fork of the Trinity. Material recovered at the sites has proved to be the oldest ever found anywhere.

But was Lewisville the site where human life first existed? Scientists don't know — too many questions remain unanswered. Now they may never be answered because waters backed up by Lewisville Dam now cover the area where many of the prehistoric hearths still lie unexplored.

HOOKED — Santa Anna, the great Mexican general, would have been jailed today as a dope addict.

Apparently he was equally addicted to women and narcotics. Along with the silk tent, silk sheets, monogrammed china and other of his memorabilia (including a solid silver thundermug) captured by Sam Houston at the Battle of San Jacinto, there also was a chest of opium. Santa Anna brought the drug along to help him make the Texas campaign more bearable.

INDIAN LORE — When the Alabama-Coushatta Indians decided to turn their East Texas reservation into a tourist attraction, they had a problem: Not one Indian knew how to build a wigwam.

Tribal fathers decided that two teepees housing guides would please the visitors. To get them built, however, they had to call in some Indians from another tribe to do the work.

Why? Because the Alabama-Coushattas are woodland Indians and they've lived in log cabins for a century or more. Most of them had never seen an authentic teepee because these were used only by Plains Indians.

THE BUFFALO SOLDIERS — For three decades following the Civil War, troops of Negro soldiers kept Texas safe from Indian attack.

Congress authorized the formation of regular Army units composed of former Negro slaves under white officers. These became the 9th and 10th Cavalry Regiments and the 24th and 25th Infantry. Both cavalry units served with distinction at Fort Davis, which still stands 25 miles from Alpine on State Highway 118.

Because of their close-curling hair, the troops were dubbed "Buffalo Soldiers" by the Indians.

WAKE OF THE BLACK WITCH — Estevan, the Moor, arrived in what now is Texas in 1528 as a slave. While attempting to find his way back home, he became the favorite medicine man of almost every Indian tribe in the area.

Estevan was the property of an officer of the ill-fated Narvaez expedition that sailed from Spain in 1527 to conquer and colonize the Gulf of Mexico. After shipwrecks and intolerable hardships, more than 80 reached what is now Galveston Island. Only four ever made it back to Mexico. This quartet included Estevan and Cabeza de Vaca.

After six years of captivity by hostile Indians, the four escaped and headed west. With a rudimentary knowledge of medicine and a little witchcraft learned from their captors, they began to practice faith-healing. And the black Estevan, the likes of whom no Indian had ever seen, became a sort of chief medicine man to the savages.

For years, Estevan remained a demi-god among the West Texas Indians. Then he returned to Mexico with his three companions. From there, the viceroy sent him back to New Mexico to look for the seven cities of gold. The Zuni Indians regarded white men as gods and reasoned that a black man was a devil. When they saw Estevan, they killed him.

TRILINGUAL — Texas' foreign heritage is so strong that official state documents used to be issued in three languages.

In 1874, the Legislature was anxious for the voters to read the full text of the annual message of Governor Richard B. Coke. They passed a resolution specifying that there would be "2,000 copies in English, 1,000 in Spanish and 1,000 in German."

A CAPITAL STATE — Texas has had more capitals than any other state or government in the western world.

Since the first Anglo-American capital was established at San Felipe de Austin, a total of seven communities have served as the capital. The others are Washington-on-the-Brazos, Harrisburg, Velasco, Columbia, Houston and Austin.

COWARD OF THE ALAMO — Louis Moses Rose, the only man who deserted rather than die at the Alamo, was to live out his life as a social outcast.

Even in a court of justice, he was to be reminded that he, alone among the 182 men in the Alamo, had traded his life for escape. Called as a witness in a murder trial at Nacogdoches on July 17, 1837, his name was listed on the record as "Luesa" — the feminine version of Louis.

It may have been a slip of the pen, but legend has it that the court clerk wrote the name that way deliberately as a reminder to all that Louis Moses Rose was a coward.

WITH A BEARD, TOO — James Butler Bonham, one of the heroes of the Alamo, was a college dropout who was expelled for demonstrating against the administration.

A native of South Carolina and the son of wealthy parents, young Jim was sent to South Carolina College (now the University) at Columbia in 1824. Two years later, disgusted with the dormitory food and unhappy with the policies of the college administration, he and another student organized a "rebellion."

In those days, college presidents took no nonsense from students. Bonham and 46 others were sent home and not allowed to reenter.

SONG OF SONGS — "The Eyes of Texas," probably the most beloved song ever written about the Lone Star State, isn't sung today as John Lang Sinclair wrote it. His original version, written on a scrap of brown laundry paper, is in the possession of The Ex-Students' Association of The University of Texas. It reads:

"The eyes of Texas are upon you
   All the live long day.
The eyes of Texas are upon you,
   They're with you all the way.
They watch you through the peaceful twilight,
   They watch you in the early dawn
When from the eastern skies the high light
   Tells that the night is gone."

EARLY BEATNIKS — Long hair for men is nothing new in Texas.

In the 1830's, long hair was the rule. When a man did pay an occasional visit to the barber, he usually asked that his shorn locks be saved. Some barbers charged extra to twist the hair into guard chains to be worn across a vest. And many a maiden swooned when her swain presented her with a ring made from a lock of his hair.

ADD HISTORY'S MYSTERIES — More than 137 years after the Texas Declaration of Independence was signed, original copies of the document are still being sought by historians.

At least six copies of the Declaration were prepared and signed by the delegates who met at Washington-on-the-Brazos on March 1, 1836. Every one of the original copies disappeared, however, and for more than 60 years, Texas did not have a single copy in its own archives.

Then, just before the turn of the century, an original copy of the Declaration was discovered in Washington and returned to Texas. However, no trace of the other copies has ever been found.

MIRRORS OF HISTORY — Through a strange quirk of fate, the wedding gift of Emperor Maximilian of Mexico to his bride, Princess Carlotta of Belgium, hangs today in a public meeting room of an Austin hotel.

The gift was eight large mirrors, each finished in gold leaf and with a bust of Carlotta on top. They were made in Maximilian's native Austria, and were intended for use by the Empress in her private quarters at Mexico City's Chapultepec Palace.

Before the mirrors were hung in the palace, however, Maximilian abdicated his throne. The wedding gift to his Empress ended up in a San Antonio antique shop.

It was there, in 1930, that Mrs. Sully Roberdeau, daughter of one of the owners of the Driskill Hotel in Austin, found them. She bought the mirrors and they hang today in the Maximilian Room on the mezzanine floor of the hotel.

NOT EVERYBODY WANTED FREEDOM — Texas did not present a united front when it decided to go to war to win its independence from Mexico. In fact, many Texans openly expressed loyalty to the Mexican government.

In 1834, when William Barret Travis and his men attacked the Mexican garrison at Anahuac, the citizens of San Felipe de Austin protested. They passed resolutions condemning the attack and reiterating their loyalty to Mexico.

The resolutions, addressed to General Cos, the Mexican commander at San Antonio, expressed the fear that such intemperate acts by Travis and his men would "endanger the entire American population of Texas."

TEXAS vs. OKLAHOMA — Texas fought its last "war" on its own soil in this century.

For nine days in July, 1931, a bridge across the Red River on Highway 75 north of Denison was the scene of a bloodless, shotless war between Texas Rangers and five companies of Oklahoma National Guardsmen.

It started when Texas built a new free bridge across the river. Owners of a parallel toll bridge objected and got an injunction which ordered the new bridge barricaded. Oklahoma ignored the court order and tore down the barricades. Texas Rangers then were sent in to keep the free bridge closed.

Oklahoma retaliated by closing its highway to the toll bridge and sending National Guardsmen to guard the road. For three days, all traffic stopped until an "armistice" was reached and both bridges were reopened.

FEUD THAT MADE A WAR — When Charles W. Jackson killed an unarmed neighbor, Joseph G. Goodbread, on a Shelbyville street in 1839, the incident set off a five-year feud remembered by history as the Regulator-Moderator War.

Jackson, fearing reprisals by Goodbread's friends, organized 150 gun-slingers into self-appointed vigilantes to "regulate" the law. Goodbread's friends, certain that law enforcement was only a farce in Shelby County, countered with a force of their own to "moderate" justice.

Not long after, the Moderators ambushed and killed Jackson. The shooting of the leader of the Regulators started the feud in earnest. During the next five years, dozens on both sides were killed by ambush or in pitched battles. Then, in 1844, President Sam Houston sent 600 militiamen into the area, rounded up the leaders of both sides and brought an end to the strangest "war" in Texas history.

BY REMOTE CONTROL — Years before the advent of radio and television, Governor James Stephen Hogg used phonograph records to address a distant audience.

On April 5, 1905, President Theodore Roosevelt was honored at the Legislative Day banquet of the State Fair of Texas and Governor Hogg was invited to speak. Illness prevented his making the trip from Austin, so he recorded his speech on ordinary phonograph records.

In those days, recordings lacked both clarity and fidelity and sound amplification systems were poor. The crowd listened attentively, however, as Governor Hogg vowed that "no graft, no crime, no public wrong shall ever stain or corrupt our state."

WAR ENDED HERE — The Civil War ended on Texas soil, not at Appamattox Courthouse in Virginia as most history books say.

On May 13, 1865 — 34 days after Lee's surrender to Grant — 1,700 Federals attacked Col. John S. (Rip) Ford's Confederates near Brownsville. The two forces skirmished all day with neither side scoring a clear victory.

That night, a Federal gunboat in the Rio Grande lobbed a shell into the Confederate camp. It caused no damage, but it angered a nameless 17-year-old Confederate who grabbed his rifle and fired back.

This was destined to be the last shot fired in the war, because both forces withdrew the next morning.

WHAT'S IN A NAME? — Texas came close to being named "Amichel."

Alonzo Alvarez de Pineda, first white man to tour Texas, proclaimed the land for Spain and named the entire Gulf coast "Amichel".

FOOTBALL PAYS — The most lucrative football game in history was played between Baylor University and the University of Houston just a decade ago.

The Houston Cougars were thrice-beaten while Baylor's Bears ranked eighth in the nation. The Baptists were such odds-on favorites that the dopesters predicted that Houston wouldn't even score. But in the first quarter, a Houston halfback led a 67-yard drive for a touchdown. By game's end, Houston had scored three more touchdowns, a field goal and a safety. Baylor had only 7 points.

In the stands that day sat Hugh Roy Cullen, Houston millionaire, who was so thrilled by "the great spirit and determination shown by the Cougars in defeating Baylor" that he gave the University of Houston $2,250,000 — an amount equal to $60,810 for every point the Cougars scored!

STORY BEHIND A PARADE — Most of the thousands who watch San Antonio's Battle of Flowers Parade each year think it commemorates a skirmish in the Texas War for Independence. It doesn't.

Sam Woolford, Alamo City historian, says it all began when President Benjamin Harrison visited San Antonio once on April 21, San Jacinto Day. The ladies of the town decided to have a parade of decorated carriages to escort the President to Alamo Plaza, but it rained and the flowers were ruined.

Several days after the President's visit, sunny skies returned and the ladies decided to have their parade anyway. When the procession ended, they began tossing their flowers to each other and soon everybody was throwing posies. Thus was born the "Battle of Flowers," now the most important parade in each year's San Jacinto celebration.

SEVEN FLAGS OVER TEXAS — Although the history books say that the flags of six different sovereign states have flown over Texas, the fact is that there have been seven.

The six flags usually associated with the history of the Lone Star State are those of Spain, France, Mexico, Texas, the Confederacy and the United States of America. But there was also a seventh flag that usually is overlooked by the historians.

It was the green, red and white flag which once flew over Laredo when that border community was the capital of the short-lived Republic of the Rio Grande.

TEXAS FIRST — It was a Texan, not Marconi, who perfected the first wireless telegraph!

In 1894, a full year before Marconi transmitted his first wireless message, Dr. Robert S. Hyer, a science professor at Southwestern University in Georgetown, transmitted wireless messages from his laboratory to the Williamson County jail — a distance of more than a mile.

However, Dr. Hyer's salary was only $130 monthly and, with a wife, two children and a mother-in-law to support, he couldn't afford to apply for a patent. By the time he was able to interest investors in his wireless, he discovered that Marconi already had patented a similar device.

ANOTHER ON THE HOUSE — Eastern visitors were unfailingly startled at the early Texans' capacity for hard liquor. In 1837, one tourist wrote:

"Nothing was regarded as a greater violation of established etiquette than for one who was going to drink not to invite all within a reasonable distance to partake, so that the Texians, being entirely a military people, not only fought but drank in platoons."

NOW IT CAN BE TOLD — Lucinda Desha Robb, first granddaughter of the late President Lyndon Johnson, was born in Maryland — but over Texas soil.

Lucinda was born in the U.S. Naval Hospital at Bethesda, Maryland, in 1968. But before she was born, her mother, Lynda Johnson Robb, made sure that the event would happen over pure Texas dirt.

Warren Woodward of Dallas, long-time Johnson family friend, had several pounds of rich Texas soil flown to Washington. Lynda had it placed under her bed in the room where Lucinda was delivered.

THE GOOD OLD DAYS? — If serious crime seems to be commonplace in Texas today, a look backward can be reassuring.

In 1870, with a population of only 818,000, Texas reported 323 murders — 195 more than any other state. Another 702 suspected murderers were being hunted by county sheriffs and town marshals.

When a suspect was arrested, holding him was a problem. Only 82 of the 158 counties had any kind of a jail. Of these, only 24 were considered secure enough to hold a dangerous prisoner.

Even when a suspect was arrested and jailed, he rarely lost his freedom for long. Time after time, gangs of citizens stormed county jails and courthouses, releasing murderers and often killing the sheriff or other officer charged with enforcing the law.

Treasure

HOOCH HOARD — Thousands of gallons of whiskey, aged for more than a century in cypress casks, await anybody who can rescue them from the Red River.

They were among the estimated 40,000 fifths of quality bourbon whiskey that were aboard the *Jim Turner*, a river steamer that piled up on a sandbar in 1854 and sank near Albion's Ferry off the town of Clarksville. Fishermen from Red River County located the rotting hulk years ago, but were never able to release it from the river's shifting sands.

As recently as 1957, the wreckage has been sighted. Over the years, many attempts have been made to salvage the cargo and a small quantity of the bourbon has been removed. Because of legal problems and the ever-changing river bed, however, nobody has been able to keep the *Jim Turner* in sight long enough to retrieve the 200 barrels of liquor known to be aboard.

NEVER SAY DIE — For almost 60 years, prospectors have searched in Stonewall County for the richest and biggest treasure hoard in all of Texas — the Spider Rock gold. One man devoted all of his money and 28 years of life to the task, but found nothing.

He was Frank Olmstead, who sold his rich Illinois farm for $500 an acre in 1920 and came to Stonewall County to look for the fabled Spanish treasure. His wife divorced him, his friends deserted him and his funds ran out — but he stayed on.

Olmstead died in 1948 without ever finding a trace of the treasure. Near his grave, 12 miles north of Aspermont, other searchers are still looking for the gold supposedly left by the Spaniards more than 200 years ago.

THE GOLD OF SAN JACINTO — Somewhere on the San Jacinto Battleground, perhaps even in the shadow of the huge monument that marks the place, there is believed to be a fortune in Mexican gold coin.

On April 21, 1836, when General Sam Houston and 783 Texans surprised the sleeping troops of the Mexican General Santa Anna and defeated them at San Jacinto, the captured Mexicans had almost no money with them.

This fact has worried historians since an army has to have money with which to buy supplies and pay the troops. The only logical explanation is that San Anna, realizing that a battle was imminent, buried the army's gold somewhere near the site where the fight took place. In fact, one of his body guards later wrote that this is exactly what happened.

At any rate, not one peso of the gold has ever been found.

TREASURE TOWN — El Paso may be the only city in the world where prospectors are still looking for a lost gold mine.

It's the Padre Mine, which legend says may contain 4,336 gold bars, 5,000 silver bars, nine mule loads of jewels that once belonged to the Aztecs and ancient manuscripts worth more than all of the other treasure put together.

The mine supposedly is on Mount Franklin, in the heart of El Paso. At least three Texans, armed with prospecting rights and considerable hope, are still looking for the mine today.

VACATION WITH PAY — The Texas Gulf Coast, especially the southern half of Padre Island, is a favorite holiday spot for amateur treasure hunters.

An estimated $15,000 in coins have been picked up along Padre beaches and probably that much more has been found and never reported. More than $2 million in gold and silver coins are known to have been on board various ships wrecked off the island, and the coins being found apparently have been washed ashore by the tides.

MONEY ISN'T EVERYTHING — Somewhere in the sand along the South Canadian River near Amarillo there is close to $10,000 in Mexican silver.

It has been there since the winter of 1832 when a band of Kiowa Indians took it from 12 Yankee traders returning home from Santa Fe. It was left there by Indian children who used the silver cartwheels as "toys."

Money was unknown to the Kiowas at the time, and they regarded their raid as a failure. They did manage to steal a few pack horses, but the silver was of little value to them. Some of the Mexican dollars were hammered into amulets for their women and

110

ornaments for their braves to wear in their hair. Most of it, however, was given to the children to play with.

LAKE OF GOLD — There's $60,000 at the bottom of Caddo Lake waiting for the treasure hunter.

It was dumped there on February 12, 1869, when the river packet *Mittie Stephens* sank just off Swanson's Landing not far from Jefferson. Of the 101 passengers aboard, 61 were lost along with $60,000 in gold.

None of the treasure has ever been recovered.

NOTE TO TREASURE HUNTERS — Hendricks Lake, in southwestern Harrison County, is known to have $2 million in pure bar silver beneath its murky waters. Only three of the bars have been recovered.

The silver is the loot of Jean Lafitte, the pirate of Galveston Island. In 1816, Lafitte took the silver from a Spanish ship, the *Santa Rosa*, in an encounter in Matagorda Bay. He then sent the treasure north to St. Louis in a wagon train mastered by one Gaspar Trammell.

Mexican officials learned of the raid and of Lafitte's plan to spirit the silver out of the country, and sent troops from San Antonio to overtake the wagon train. The soldiers caught up with Trammell at Hendricks Lake, but before they could capture the loot, the wily wagon master shoved the six treasure-laden freighters into the water. They sank, and the silver has never been recovered.

In the 1920's, three of the silver bars were accidentally hauled to the surface of the lake by fishermen. The rest of the $2 million, however, has defied treasure-seekers to this day.

PEARLS FOR THE PICKING — Caddo Lake, in northeastern Harrison County, is one of the few places in the U.S. where pearls can be had for the taking.

The lake abounds with fresh-water mussel which produce a natural pearl only slightly below the quality found in oysters. The pearl-bearing mussel are found in shallow water, so no diving is required.

In the early years of this century, pearl hunting at Caddo Lake was so profitable that hundreds of Texans camped on the shores for months at a time. Some of the luckier pearl hunters made as much as $3,000 in a year.

Development of the cultured variety by the Japanese made pearl hunting unprofitable, but the mussel — and the pearls — are still in Caddo Lake.

FOOTNOTE TO HISTORY — The wealth of an army lies buried a few miles northeast of Brownsville in the verdant Rio

Grande Valley.

It was buried there on May 8-9, 1846, during the Mexican War. Troops led by General Zachary Taylor attacked a contingent of General Santa Anna's army a few miles east of Los Fresnos. Although outnumbered, the Americans defeated the Mexicans handily.

As the Mexicans began retreating, they buried their personal jewelry, money and the loot they had taken in previous battles. The hiding place was on the south bank of the Resaca de la Palma. The troop pay wagons, each loaded with Spanish gold coins, were buried on the battlefield itself.

For almost a century and a quarter, treasure hunters have looked for the sites. They have never been found.

Traveling Texas

FIRST TOURIST? — Outsiders have been traveling to Texas since 1519!

It was only 27 years after Columbus discovered America that Alonzo Alvarez de Pineda, the Spanish explorer, visited and mapped the Texas Gulf Coast. Nine years after Pineda's visit, Cabeza de Vaca and a group of companions landed on what is now Galveston Island. Tourists have been coming to Texas in increasing numbers ever since.

LAND OF SKY BLUE WATER? — Texas has more inland water than any state except Alaska. Minnesota, the "land of lakes," is third.

FERRY TALE — Los Ebanos, in Hidalgo County, is the only place where a person can leave or enter the United States on a hand-pulled ferry.

Located a few miles off U.S. Highway 83 at the end of Farm Road 886, the ferry charges 50 cents per car to shunt passengers between the U.S. and Mexico. The rickety ferry is powered by four Mexicans who literally pull it to and fro across the river with ropes.

IT'S A FACT — There are two long stretches of Texas highways where it is easy for motorists to run out of gas.

There isn't a service station anywhere on the 57-mile stretch of U.S. Highway 77 that crosses the King Ranch between Riviera and Raymondville. And there is neither a rest room nor a gasoline pump along the 63 miles of U.S. 59 between Freer and Laredo.

GIGANTIC GOOF — Texas boasts what might be the world's biggest bathtub, but it won't hold water.

Alongside Interstate 20, in the southeast edge of Monahans in far West Texas, there is a concrete bowl that is 522 feet long and 425 feet wide. It was put there in 1928 by the Shell Oil Co. and was designed as a unit where a million barrels of oil could be stored while awaiting shipment by tank cars or pipelines.

The only problem was that the oil wouldn't stay put. The hot sun evaporated it. The pressure on the concrete walls and floor was such that thousands of gallons seeped out. Despite these problems, however, the company continued to use the bowl for several years until pipelines could be built.

Later Shell sold the tank to a Monahans man who hoped to turn it into a recreation lake. But the water seeped out, too.

RESERVATIONS, PLEASE — For as little as $6 a night, the visitor to Jefferson, in deep East Texas, can stay in a hotel boasting chandeliers and paintings from France, fireplace mantels of Italian marble and a ballroom whose columns once graced a Grecian hillside.

It's the Excelsior House, which has been accepting guests now since the 1850's. Today it is owned and operated by the ladies of the Jessie Allen Wise Garden Club who do all of the work of running it.

Guests willing to pay a little more than the standard $6 to $15 rates may occupy the two-room Presidential Suite where both Presidents Grant and Hayes rested while visiting Jefferson.

JOKER'S WILD — Greenhorns making their first trip West usually lost their appetites when their stagecoach made an overnight stop at Nimitz's famous hotel in Fredericksburg, Gillespie County.

It wasn't because Charles H. Nimitz, who built the hotel in 1852, didn't set a fine table, because it was famous for its food. And the pungent smell of meat being cured over oak coals in the smokehouse behind the hotel invariably greeted the arriving traveler and made him ravenous.

If the tenderfoot tarried in the hotel lobby before going to the dining room, however, he usually skipped the meal. That was because the local loafers who gathered there liked to tell travelers that Fredericksburg had no embalmer and that Nimitz used the smokehouse to cure corpses. They would swear that at that very moment a deceased hotel guest was being prepared for his final journey.

HOW IT BEGAN — San Antonio's Menger Hotel was built because a local brewer needed a place to house his customers overnight.

William Menger began brewing beer in the Alamo City in the mid-1840's and his product was so good that distributors came from all over to buy it. He developed so much business from nearby German settlements that he had to have a place to house visiting buyers.

He acquired a lot across from the Alamo and built the Menger Hotel in 1859. It is still one of San Antonio's leading inns.

IT COULD ONLY HAPPEN HERE — One of Lubbock's top tourist attractions is, of all things, a bank. It's the only spot on the High Plains where a visitor, in a one-hour conducted tour, can get a good look at paintings, sculpture and *objects d'art* from around the world.

Lubbock's First National Bank has more than 500 pieces of art collected from galleries and individuals in London, Paris, Athens, Madrid and a dozen other faraway places. In addition, it boasts many sculptures and paintings commissioned by the bank from artists whose works are well known.

Each department of the bank from the offices of the board chairman (Southwestern decor) to the data processing division (Ancient Egypt) is decorated with authentic art from different countries of the world and different periods. Viewing these art treasures has become so popular that the bank has trained guides to take visitors on complete tours.

THE FLAG IS STILL THERE — Most residents have never seen it, but the city of Houston has an official flag that never flies except in the chambers of the City Council.

Houston's flag is a white star on a navy blue background. In the center of the star, a double banded ring of red surrounds a depiction of the official seal of the city. The seal bears a drawing of a locomotive with a star above it and a plow below it.

Unlike Denison, in Grayson County, which flies its city flag daily from a pole located at its busiest intersection, Houston never hails its banner in public.

WHERE PRESIDENTS ARE REMEMBERED — Franklin Delano Roosevelt's old "shooting stick seat" that the crippled president used to prop himself into a sitting position reposes today in a unique museum in Odessa.

Known simply as the Presidential Museum, the collection was started by John Ben Shepperd, former attorney general of Texas. His purpose: "To bring about a better understanding of, and respect for, the Presidency . . . to depict in a positive manner the fact that the Presidency of the United States is a great and noble responsibility."

Today the museum has on display more than 2,500 original documents and personal effects representing each of the 37 men who have served in the nation's highest office. The collection ranges from the buttons from one of George Washington's uniforms to a favorite red parasol that belonged to F.D.R.

HE OWNS IT — What may be the state's only privately-owned fort is a few miles off Interstate 10 in Hudspeth County.

A few years ago, Tom Powell found a set of plans for the construction of Fort Quitman, which used to guard the Rio Grande not far from the present town of Sierra Blanca. He has spent thousands of dollars restoring the old fort.

TINIEST PARK — Acton State Park, at the intersection of Highways 208 and 190 in Hood County, is only 12 feet wide and 21 feet long!

Probably the smallest state park in America, it is a memorial to Elizabeth Patton Crockett and Robert Crockett, wife and son of Davy Crockett, hero of the Alamo.

IT IS STARTED IN COURT — Canton's famed "First Monday," a monthly outdoor shop-and-swap fair that has become one of the largest community trading markets in the U.S., had its beginnings in a courtroom!

On the first Monday in December, 1848, a circuit judge arrived in Canton to hold his first court. Since there was no courthouse, he ordered chairs and benches set out under a tree. Two farmers waiting for court to convene began discussing their favorite horses. After much discussion, they decided to swap even.

Horse-trading continued thereafter on each circuit court day, which happened to be the first Monday of each month. Soon it became a major attraction in Canton.

Today "First Monday" (actually Sunday and Monday) draws some 800 dealers in almost everything to the Van Zandt County town. As many as 10,000 prospective buyers sometimes show up.

TEXAS FIRST — In 1930, State Highway Engineer Gibb Gilchrist told contractors building new roads to save trees whenever possible and to watch for sites that might be used for roadside parks.

Most of the engineers, who liked to save money by building roads arrow-straight, thought that Gilchrist was crazy. They followed orders, however, and even went so far as to put some picnic benches and tables beneath some live oak trees alongside State Highway 71 in Fayette County.

Thus was established the first roadside park in Texas — the beginning of a system of more than 840,000 acres of grass, trees and wildflowers maintained along state highways today.

INN OF DISTINCTION — San Antonio's St. Anthony Hotel was the first hostelry in the world to be completely air-conditioned, the first to have a drive-in motor entrance where guests could register and go directly to their rooms and the first to have both a tub and shower in every room.

Built in 1909, the St. Anthony also is one of the few hotels in the world that has an original oil or water color painting by a famous artist in each of its 550 rooms. And each room, incidentally, is decorated entirely differently from any of the others.

No wonder the St. Anthony, New York's Waldorf-Astoria and San Francisco's Fairmont have been voted by a national travel writers organization as America's only three truly distinctive hotels that are more than 50 years old.

BELIEVE-IT-OR-NOT — One of the shortest state highways in the U.S. is located near downtown Austin.

It is State Highway 165, and is only .8 of a mile in length. It is located wholly within the State Cemetery in the capital city.

State 165 also was the first Texas highway to be named for a living person. Known as "Lou Kemp Drive," it honors the man responsible for locating the graves of many prominent Texans and arranging to have their bodies reburied in the State Cemetery.

WELL, NOW — San Augustine residents often drop into Stripling's Drug Store for nothing more than a drink of water.

The old town well, dug more than a century ago by slave labor, is inside the store. Stripling, who has been doing business at the same spot for more than 70 years, believes that his is the only pharmacy in the U.S. with a water well as a part of its equipment.

TOWN THAT REMEMBERS — At the intersection of U.S. 85 and 385 in Dalhart, Dallam-Hartley Counties, the cowboys who used to ride for the old XIT Ranch are memorialized in a monument that is topped with an empty saddle.

It all started three decades ago when John Marsh of Miles City, Montana, a retired line rider on the big ranch, was planning to return to Dalhart for the annual XIT Reunion. He died, however, before the reunion came off, and his widow asked if a horse with an empty saddle could be led in the parade in memory of her dead husband.

Each year since, a riderless horse has been a part of the XIT Reunion parade in memory of those cowboys who have gone to the last roundup. And Dalhart, adopting the riderless horse as a sort of civic trademark, had the empty saddle monument executed and installed at the highway intersection.

WHERE THE STARS FELL — Ten minutes from downtown Odessa is one of the rarest sights in the world — a series of meteor craters.

The Odessa craters, created about 20,000 years ago when a shower of meteorites struck the earth, are among the less than two dozen such sites known to exist on the earth. Discovered in 1892, the largest crater is about 550 feet in diameter and 100 feet deep.

Nearby are smaller craters ranging in size from 15 to 70 feet in diameter and from seven to 18 feet in depth.

DOWN MEMORY LANE — At a roadside park on Farm Road 302, west of Mentone, Loving County, the traveler can still see the deep tracks cut by stagecoaches as they passed by on the old Butterfield Trail.

FANTASTIC FANDANGLE — A $40 production staged by high school seniors to raise money for a class trip was the beginning of one of the most unusual theatrical productions in the U.S.

It is the Fort Griffin Fandangle, staged each year in the Shackelford County town of Albany (pop. 2,000). This show, which usually plays a six-night stand, includes a cast of 300 and is staged in a natural hillside theater seating 1,600. The script is taken from the county history and the story, music and acting all are by local talent.

The Fandangle had its beginnings in 1938 when the Albany High School senior class decided to stage a homemade production to raise funds for a graduation trip to Carlsbad Caverns. A teacher named Bob Nail wrote and produced the show for about $40.

The effort was so successful that Nail continued writing a new script each year, using old newspaper files, history books and the recollections of pioneers as his source. The Fort Griffin Fandangle (named after the historic old army installation nearby) was the result.

Nail died in 1968, but his associates continue to write the show.

PRIVATE HOLIDAY — Seymour, the Baylor County seat, celebrates May Day in a special way: It closes up!

It started three decades ago when Lake Kemp was built nearby and there was a closed season to allow the fish to multiply. The lake was opened on May 1, and virtually every citizen of Seymour dutifully closed shop and went fishing.

They've been doing it each year since and May 1 is regarded as a local holiday.

SEE IT TO BELIEVE IT — Don't try it without a guide, but the interior of the Big Thicket offers more beauty and pure adventure per square foot than almost any spot left in America.

Within the remaining 300,000 acres of this remarkable East Texas wilderness (there were 3.2 million acres originally) one can walk through palmetto forests so high that they swallow a man on horseback. At least 21 varieties of wild orchids bloom beneath the pines — only two of the 67 recognized species of trees and shrubs to be found there.

The black bear and panther have been destroyed by hunters, but mink, otter and muskrat abound along the streams. So do foxes, wolves, wild hogs and dozens of other species of wildlife.

If you're planning a visit to the Big Thicket, however, you'd better hurry. It's disappearing at the rate of 50 acres per day!

FOR MEMBERS ONLY — One of the best museums in Texas is not a museum at all but a Monahans club.

In the late 1930's, Joe Farr began collecting every authentic relic he could find. These range from what is probably the best private collection of Indian artifacts in the Southwest to the world's first known vacuum cleaner. Included are priceless statuary and paintings as well as music boxes and nickelodeons from Mississippi River boats.

Farr displays the stuff at his J & J Club in Monahans, in deep West Texas.

THE PASSING PARADE — Shot towers, those unique structures that were built during the Civil War for the manufacture of lead bullets, have all but disappeared in Texas. However, at least one still stands in Erath County not far from Dublin.

These stone towers, from four to six feet in diameter and from 25 to 35 feet high, look like tall chimneys. They were designed this way to create a strong updraft. When molten lead was poured in drops from the top of the tower shaft, the draft of air caused it to congeal into spheres or balls. These fell into a water vat at ground level and hardened.

The size of the shot (which ranged from pellets to small cannonballs) was determined by the amount of molten lead poured from the top and by the distance it fell before reaching the vat. Making ammunition in this way was a small, but important, industry in Texas until the war ended in 1865.

NUTTY NOTE — Unnoticed by most travelers on Interstate 20, a lone pecan tree — protected by a wire enclosure — stands five miles east of Putnam, between Abilene and Cisco.

It happend to be the world's first tree to produce the Burkett pecan. J. H. Burkett found an unusual variety of the nut growing along Battle Creek, took a bud from it and produced one of the first thin-shelled pecans ever grown. Today the Burkett is one of the most popular varieties of pecans on the market.

TEXAS BRAG — Baylor University at Waco houses the world's largest and most complete collection of the works and memorabilia of the English husband-and-wife poetry team of Elizabeth Barrett and Robert Browning.

Notable Browning collections are owned by Oxford University in England, the British Museum, the Library of Congress and the New York Public Library. All of them combined, however, cannot match the contents of Baylor's Browning Library, put together over a lifetime by Professor A. Joseph Armstrong.

WHAT'S IN A NAME? — Pasadena, the Harris County city that depends on miles of smelly oil refineries and petro-chemical plants for its livelihood, was planned as a city of gracious homes where the air always would be pure.

J. H. Burnet, the Georgia native who founded the town, named it after Pasadena, Calif., because he hoped to build a beautiful city like that on the Texas Gulf Coast. The name Pasadena, freely translated, means "passing through pleasant grounds."

LITTLE ITALY — If the traveler along the Brazos River bottoms in Brazos, Robertson and Burleson Counties begins to wonder if he is in Italy instead of Texas, there's a reason: More than 600 families of Sicilian descent operate farms in the area.

They've been farming in Texas since 1875 when the first group came over from Sicily.

NO COLOR LINE — Nacogdoches may have the only monument ever erected by white citizens to honor a runaway slave.

He was William Goyens, a mulatto who migrated to East Texas from his native South Carolina in 1821 after escaping from the plantation where he was a slave. He amassed a small fortune as a Nacogdoches land dealer, wagon manufacturer and machine shop owner. Goyens acquired some slaves of his own, but also employed white men in his business enterprises.

In 1936, the Texas Centennial Commission put up the monument which recounts the highlights of his career and ends with the words:
"His skin was black,
His heart true blue."

ODD TEXAS — Kenedy County, although larger than the state of Rhode Island, hasn't a single commercial business within its borders.

More than 900 people live there and it has a county seat town — Sarita. But except for a post office, school, church and a commissary that supplies a few staples to the residents who work on the King

Ranch, there are no other businesses.

It's the only county in Texas that doesn't even have a gasoline station.

GOOFY GEOGRAPHY — It's possible to get from Texas to New Mexico by traveling in any direction.

The catch, however, is that there is just one starting-point from which this is possible. In the desert west of El Paso and south of Interstate 10, there's a spot where the border of Texas makes a slight dip. From that little semi-circle, New Mexico is north, south, east and west of Texas.

Proof? Look at the El Paso area inset on the Texas Highway Department map.

SAVIOUR'S STORE — For 51 years, Jesus Christ was the sole owner of an unusual store at Waller, northwest of Houston.

Mr. and Mrs. A. D. Purvis founded God's Mercy Store and operated it until a few years ago. They didn't own the store, however. In 1916, they deeded the property to Jesus Christ "for and in consideration of the love that we have for Him."

During the years that they operated the store, Mr. and Mrs. Purvis sold all merchandise at cost. They asked only that their customers add a ten per cent "tip" as their "profit."

ONE OF A KIND — Serbin, in southern Lee County, is one of two Wendish settlements remaining in the world. (The other is in Australia).

Wends are Germans of Slavic descent who emigrated from southeast Germany in 1854 and settled in more than a dozen communities in Texas. Except for the village of Serbin, however, the Wends (or Serbs, as they prefer to be called) have no recognizeable settlement left in the state.

DRIVERS' BOOK — In the early days of motoring in Texas, each county clerk kept a careful record of every driver and his automobile.

The law required each driver to appear annually at the county clerk's office, write his name in a registration book kept for the purpose and receive a number assigned by the county. The cost? Only fifty cents a year!

OLDEST ROAD — Texas may have been tourist-minded in 1844 when the Republic's Congress took bids on the "Central National Road." This road began on the Red River, near where Denison now stands, and ran south to Galveston Bay. One stipulation to bidders was that no stump in the finished road could be more than 12 inches high! The "Central National Road" now is U.S. Highway 75.

FOREST OF LILLIPUT — Whoever said "you can't see the forest for the trees" had never been to Texas.

A few miles east of Monahans, in West Texas, there's a forest that covers hundreds of acres — but you can look right over the tree tops. The tallest tree is only 30 inches high.

It is the largest stand of miniature Harvard oaks left in the U.S. The Lilliputian forest is in Sandhills State Park, a 4,000-acre sweep of pure white sand that lies between Monahans and Odessa.

GOLDEN ROAD — Portions of two Texas highways are actually paved with gold!

In 1936, when U.S. Highways 81 and 287 were being built across Montague County in north Texas, construction workers noticed that the sand being used to mix the concrete glistened. When a sample was sent to a Fort Worth laboratory to be assayed, it was found to contain fifty-four cents worth of gold per ton of ore.

Recovering the gold was not commercially feasible, however, and eventually $37,000 worth of it — all imbedded in the sand — became a part of 39 miles of highway.

IT'S THE LAW! — If you're a male between the ages of 21 and 45, a Texas resident and in good health, watch out. You can be called upon to work five days at hard labor on your county's roads!

In 1876, the Legislature passed a law requiring all males (except preachers) to work at least five days a year on county roads. The law is still on the books, but it hasn't been invoked for many years.

THE BELL TOLD — Texas' first traffic law, passed in 1907, required motor vehicles to have a bell or other appliance that would give notice of their approach.

Speed within towns was limited to a slow eight miles per hour, but 18 was legal on the open road. Horses — if they had a rider or driver — had right of way over all vehicles.

ROYAL ROAD — Like old roads? In Texas, it's possible to travel a highway first opened to traffic more than 300 years ago.

State Highway 21, between Crockett and Alto in Houston and Cherokee Counties, is one of the longest still used segments of *El Camino Real*, first designated a highway by the King of Spain in 1689.

122

The King's Highway, which once crossed Texas to connect Mexico City and the French settlements in Louisiana, is the nation's oldest long-distance roadway still surviving much of its original route.

People and Politics

THE COMFORTS OF HOME — For more than 30 years, Governors of Texas had to leave their residence to take a bath.

When the Executive Mansion was built in 1855, the only bathroom was a lean-to outside the main building. It was finally moved inside in the 1870's, but it was not until 1913 that additional bathrooms were added.

FROM LAWYER TO PRESIDENT — A couple of murderers were inadvertently responsible for naming the first president of the Republic of Texas.

They were John and William Smith, and they had been convicted and sentenced to hard labor by the court at Liberty. Their attorney, however, hoped to get their sentence commuted, and he came to Washington-on-the-Brazos on March 11, 1836, to plead their case before the convention assembled there.

When the attorney, David G. Burnet arrived at Washington, he found that the convention was divided over the election of a president. Would he permit his name to be put up as a compromise candidate?

He agreed, and on March 16, 1836, Burnet — who didn't even have a vote himself in the convention — was elected president of Texas.

HEROES MADE MONEY, TOO — Ben Milam and James Bowie, later to become heroes at the Alamo, pocketed some of the profits in Texas' first land scandal.

In 1835, the legislature of the Mexican states of Coahuila and Texas, fearing the rise of Santa Anna to power, decided to sell some of the public lands to raise money for defense. The law permitted individuals in Texas to buy up to 400 leagues of land (about 2 million acres) for as little as seven cents an acre.

Milan, Bowie and Samuel Williams, then the private secretary to Stephen F. Austin, were among those who profited from the land speculations before the Mexican government declared the law invalid.

DID NEW DEAL BEGIN HERE? — Did President Franklin D. Roosevelt's "New Deal" originate in Texas instead of the White House?

It may have. In 1912, Col. Edward M. House of Austin, advisor and close friend of President Woodrow Wilson, wrote a novel. It was called *Philip Dru: Administrator, A Story of Tomorrow, 1920-35.* In the story, House advocated such revolutionary new ideas as social security, government works projects, retirement of Supreme Court justices at 70, a "brain trust" to advise the President, workmen's compensation insurance and others which were to become a part of F.D.R.'s "New Deal."

Roosevelt read the novel shortly after it was published and was impressed by it. He and House remained friends, and the Texan was a frequent White House visitor in the early days of Roosevelt's presidency. Whether or not the novel actually inspired the New Deal, however, is a matter for historians to ponder.

KEYS TO THE KINGDOM — Once a Governor of Texas leaves office, he literally throws away the keys. New locks are installed immediately on all Capitol doors each time an administration changes.

Even this security wasn't enough to satisfy the late W. Lee O'Daniel when he was governor from 1939 to 1941. To protect his private office from any unwarranted interruption, O'Daniel had an electric lock installed which he alone could operate by flipping a button on his desk.

THE RULING CLASS — Counting the five presidents of the Republic, a total of 98 men and one woman have been chief executives of Texas.

The first governor was Don Domingo Teran de los Rios, named in 1691 by the King of Spain. He was followed by a succession of 36 others who governed Texas for Spain until Mexico gained control of the territory in 1822. There were 15 Mexican governors of Texas.

Henry Smith was named the provisional colonial governor in 1835, just before independence. He was impeached and James W. Robinson served as acting governor until the Republic was a reality and a president elected.

Between independence and statehood, the Republic of Texas elected five presidents but only four men served. Sam Houston served two non-consecutive terms, having been elected the second and fourth president of the Republic.

Since annexation by the United States in 1845, Texas has had 4 occupants of the governor's office. One of these was Mrs. Miriam A. Ferguson, the only woman ever to govern Texas. She occupied the office for two non-consecutive terms.

THE CHICKEN SALAD CASE — It took the Supreme Court to decide who has to pay for any chicken salad the Governor of Texas may decide to serve at the Executive Mansion.

On February 11, 1915, the Legislature appropriated $2,000 per year for two years to cover expenditures for fuel, lights, water, ice and food (including chicken salad and punch) which O. B. Colquitt had incurred during his term as governor. The Attorney General took a look at the appropriation and ruled that it was invalid.

Eventually the case went to the Supreme Court. The judges ruled that the Legislature could appropriate for utilities and ice at the Mansion, but that groceries like chicken salad had to be paid for by the Governor.

IT TAKES ALL KINDS — In the mid 1930's, the Grayson County town of Collinsville decided to honor its most famous son, William H. (Alfalfa Bill) Murray, then governor of Oklahoma. They put up a 20-foot-high granite pile in the town square and invited Murray down to dedicate it.

Murray, author of the Oklahoma state constitution and a brilliant legislator, also was an unpredictable eccentric. He claimed (correctly) that he was not born in Collinsville, but in Toadsuck, a settlement that antedated the present town. He apparently resented the efforts of Collinsville to claim him as a native.

At any rate, he drove down from Oklahoma City in his black limousine for the dedication of the monument. When he arrived, however, he refused to make a speech and finally drove off in a huff. Collinsville citizens, irate at Alfalfa Bill's response, eventually removed the monument.

PROMOTION NOTIONS — In 1944, when President Franklin D. Roosevelt was looking for a likely place from which to launch the "March of Dimes" campaign for that year, he picked the Lee County town of Dime Box.

The place came by its unique name many years before. Early settlers used to impose on the postman to pick up supplies for them at the nearest settlement. In appreciation, they began leaving a dime in the mailbox for his trouble. When a post office was opened, it was called Dime Box.

TEXAS FIRST? — Austin's courthouse historian, Weldon Hart, says that Sam Houston may have been the first Texan to express concern about water pollution.

After he was baptized in 1854 in the waters of Rock Creek, he was asked if all of his sins had been washed away.

"I hope so," General Houston replied, "but if they were all washed away, the Lord help the fish down below."

WELCOME STRANGER — Texas' 18-room Executive Mansion has only one bedroom for guests.

It's the Sam Houston Room. Furnishings include the massive canopied four-poster bed which Houston ordered made for his personal use from East Texas pine.

TEXAS FACT — Beauford H. Jester, who died July 11, 1949, of a heart attack while traveling from Austin to Houston on a train, is the only Texas governor to die while in office.

THREE'S A CROWD — Two of the three candidates for president of the Republic of Texas in 1838 killed themselves before election day.

James Collinsworth jumped off a boat in Galveston Bay. Peter W. Grayson, en route home from Washington where he had been sent on a mission for the Republic, shot himself in Tennessee.

Mirabeau B. Lamar, the third candidate, survived the campaign and was elected by an almost unanimous vote.

CIVIL WAR AMONG POLITICIANS — In 1873, Democrats and Republicans almost had a shooting war over which party would control the government of Texas.

Hostilities began after Democrat Richard Coke trounced Edmund J. Davis, the Republic governor and his Carpetbag government, in the elections of 1873. Davis, however, decided that he wanted to stay in office and he had his rubber-stamp Supreme Court declare the elections unconstitutional.

Ignoring the court's decision, Coke and the members of the new 14th Legislature arrived in Austin after New Year's Day prepared to take their posts. They discovered that the Governor and members of the preceding Legislature planned to hold onto their offices by force. Through a ruse, however, Coke and the new legislators got control of the House and Senate chambers in the capitol, swore themselves in and settled down to work.

Governor Davis and the 13th Legislature had control of the first floor of the capitol and they refused to let Coke and the Democrats leave. For two days, Texas had two governors and two Legislatures with each group operating as an armed camp on different floors of the capitol. The Davis forces finally capitulated on January 17, 1874, and Carpetbag rule ended in Texas.

ONE WAY OUT — Once when a Texas congressman disagreed with a ruling by the Speaker, he showed his displeasure by kicking out a door in the U.S. House of Representatives.

It happened in January, 1890, when Speaker Thomas B. Reed of Maine ordered all doors locked to keep members of the House in their places during a vote. Representative Constantine Buckley Kilgore of Wills Point responded by announcing that he intended to leave the chamber anyway.

When he found the exit from the House not only locked but with a guard barring the way, he pushed the guard aside, kicked out the door panels and left. Since then the House rules have been rewritten so that any member who defies the Speaker can be arrested by the sergeant-at-arms.

HOGG VS. HOUSTON — Andrew Jackson Houston, youngest son of the hero of San Jacinto, ran for public office only once. He was badly beaten.

Houston, a Republican, hoped that James Stephen Hogg could be defeated in his bid for re-election as governor in 1892. The Democrats had split and nominated a fusion candidate to run against Hogg. The Populists also named a strong contender. But the Republicans decided not to oppose the governor at all.

Angered. Houston staged a rump Republican convention and got himself nominated — but it was a lost cause. Hogg led the ticket with 190,000-plus votes and his two major opponents polled more than 100,000 ballots each. Houston, whose name failed to excite the electorate as his father's had, got only 1,312 votes.

Although he never sought public office again, Houston died a U.S. Senator. He was past 80 when Governor W. Lee O'Daniel appointed him to serve out an unexpired term in the 1940's. Houston died before the term ended.

MURDER UNDER THE DOME — Robbery, not political revenge, was the motive for the only assassination to occur on the steps of the State Capitol in Austin.

Louis Francke, a member of the House of Representatives from Fayette, had stopped by the office of the House Sergeant-at-Arms on February 19, 1873, to pick up his *per diem* and travel reimbursement as the Legislature neared adjournment. Then he had gone gown to a Congress Avenue saloon, ordered a beer and paid for it with a large bill.

Returning to the Capitol about 7 p.m., Representative Francke was attacked by two men who apparently were lying in wait for him on the steps near the main entrance. He was beaten about the head with a rock, robbed and tossed down the entrance steps. He died a few hours later.

Although a number of witnesses had noticed two strange men on the Capitol steps and a grocer nearby remembered selling them some beer, they were never apprehended.

POLITICAL PALAVER — David G. Burnet, provisional president of the Republic of Texas, and Sam Houston, commander-in-chief of the Army, had a lasting dislike for each other. Their relations did not improve with time.

Nine years after independence was won, Burnet wrote:

"Sam Houston has been generally proclaimed the hero of San Jacinto. No fiction of the novelist is farther from the truth. Houston was the only man on the battlefield who deserved censure.

"The army regarded him as a military fop, and the citizens were disgusted at his miserable imbecility. But when wounded, he visited New Orleans as a hero . . . and accounts of his reception were circulated throughout Texas. A complete reaction set in, and Sam Houston . . . never worthy to be called a brave man or a wise man, became the hero of San Jacinto and the Second President of the Republic."

BIG MAN IN THE CAPITOL — Richard B. Hubbard, who weighed in at more than 300 pounds, was the heaviest man ever to serve as governor of Texas.

LOST GRAVE — Pendleton Murrah is the only former governor of Texas whose exact burial place is not known.

Murrah was governor from November, 1863, until the break-up of the Confederacy in 1865. Following the surrender of the Confederate armies, he sought refuge in Mexico and died the same year in Monterrey. He was buried there, but the location of his grave is unknown.

AUTO-BIOGRAPHY — A Packard Twin-Six automobile played a starring role in the lives of two Texas governors.

It was in the Packard that Governor and Mrs. James E. Ferguson, the shadow of impeachment upon them, drove away from the Executive Mansion in Austin in the fall of 1917. Mrs. Ferguson was driving, and as they left the grounds, she assured her husband that someday the same car would bring them back to occupy the mansion again.

Two years later, the Packard — its tires worn thin and its engine in need of major repair — was stored in a Temple garage. And there it remained until November, 1924, when Texas voters elected Mrs. Ferguson to the office from which her husband had been removed.

Remembering her prediction of seven years before, Mrs. Ferguson took the Packard out of storage and had it repaired and polished. And on January 19, 1924, the governor-elect, with her husband at her side, drove the Packard Twin-Six back to Austin for her own inauguration.

HOT POLITICS — During its first 62 years as the official residence of the Governor of Texas, the Executive Mansion in Austin was heated only by open fireplaces. In 1917, when the wife of Governor W. P. Hobby asked that steam heat be installed, advisors warned that such fancy plumbing might hurt her husband's political career.

"I had rather be warm for two years than freeze for four," she replied. And the steam boiler was installed.

THE GIFT NOBODY WANTED — Had Sam Houston accepted a gift offered him in 1836, Texas would have been the only State in the Union without any form of taxation.

In that year, Samuel F. B. Morse offered his invention of the telegraph as a gift to the Republic of Texas. Houston not only didn't accept it, but failed even to acknowledge Morse's letter. Finally, 20 years later, Morse wrote Houston that "I am induced to believe that . . . (the) gift . . . was of no value to the State" and withdrew his offer.

One statistician has deduced that the telegraph would have earned enough in royalties to have paid all costs of state government and, at the same time, created a reserve fund of many millions of dollars. The state treasury would have been so rich that Texas wouldn't have had to levy a single tab of any kind!

COME ONE, COME ALL — In the early days of statehood, Texas governors followed a policy of keeping their office doors open at all times and any citizen who wanted an audience needed only to walk in unannounced.

By the time Sam Houston became governor, the burdens of the office had reached such proportions that he found it impossible to see every visitor. He announced that after May 1, 1860, he would see citizens by appointment only. Editorial writers on most state papers criticized Houston for his "undemocratic action," but it is a policy that has been followed by all governors since.

TOGA TOO TIGHT — Tennessee turned down the chance to own Sam Houston's favorite portrait of himself because state officials felt that it was indecent.

In 1831, Houston commissioned Washington Cooper to paint him garbed in the toga of a Roman senator and standing among the ruins of Carthage. The painting, which Houston preferred over all others, eventually came into the possession of Judge A. W. Terrell of Austin.

Thinking the people of Tennessee would like to have the favorite picture of their former governor, Judge Terrell offered it to the state. Officials rejected the offer because of what they termed Houston's "immodest" dress.

In 1910, Orlando Rouland made an enlarged copy of painting for the Texas Senate. The original is in the University of Texas at Austin Academic Center.

OF HATS AND PRESIDENTS — Lyndon Johnson may have made the ten-gallon hat stylish the world over, but it was another Texas president who named it and made it standard headgear for Southwestern dudes.

In 1836, Sam Houston purchased his first Texas-made hat in the city that bears his name. He put it on the shelf until after he won the Battle of San Jacinto. Later, as president of the Republic of Texas, old Sam wore what he described as "my ten-gallon hat" on all public occasions.

It wasn't long until almost every man in Texas had his own ten-gallon hat, and except for changes in size and style, it has continued to be worn since.

POLITICIAN'S DREAM — Sam Houston would have been welcomed as a candidate by any political party. He probably held more different public offices than any man in history.

A native of Virginia, he moved to Tennessee where he was elected to Congress and then Governor. Moving on to Texas, he was twice elected president of the Republic. When Texas joined the Union, he was elected U.S. Senator, then returned to serve as Governor.

THE TRAGEDY OF ANSON JONES — Dr. Anson Jones, last president of the Republic of Texas, died a suicide.

Elected president in 1844, he presided over the annexation of Texas by the United States, then retired from politics and went to live on his Washington County farm. Public life still lured him, however, and he ran for the U.S. Senate in 1857. He was defeated.

A few months later, on January 9, 1858, he ecountered a friend in the old Capitol Hotel in Houston, site of the first Texas Capitol. "Here in this house 20 years ago, I began my political career as a member of the Texas Senate," he said, "Here I would like to close it."

He then went to his room and shot himself.

MR. PRESIDENT — Jean Lafitte, the pirate, was the first "President of Texas" — by his own proclamation.

When he moved his headquarters and almost a thousand villainous buccaneers from Louisiana to Texas and set up his new lair at Galveston in 1817, he proclaimed to all that he was "President of Texas."

His "presidency" lasted only three years. He and his freebooters sailed away from Galveston in 1820, and some historians believe the old pirate retired to a life of respectability.

SOCIAL NOTE — When the Governor of Texas entertains his personal friends at the Executive Mansion, he has to pay for the food and drink. And if he sends out invitations, he pays for them, too.

The Legislature makes an annual appropriation for the upkeep of the Executive Mansion and for official entertaining. However, the courts have held that when the Governor has a few friends in for lunch or an evening of bridge, he has to pick up the tab himself.

DID YOU KNOW? — Edmund J. Davis, probably the most disliked and most feared governor of Texas, has the most imposing monument on the highest point in the State Cemetery at Austin.

Davis was the "scalawag" governor of Reconstruction days and was virtually dictator of Texas from 1869 until he was defeated by Richard Coke in 1873. Although despised as chief executive, Davis was respected and generally liked by those who knew him as a private citizen.

THE CHANGING TIMES — Candidates for public office today woo voters from special trains, helicopters and jet planes, but the second governor of Texas won election on muleback.

George Tyler Wood not only rode his mule, Pantellete, into the office of governor, but she continued to be his favorite transportation after his election. Governor Wood also kept the common touch by always refusing to wear socks.

RARELY-TOLD-TALE — Health, not the search for wealth, brought some of history's great names to Texas.

Mirabeau B. Lamar and Dr. Anson Jones, both destined to be president of the Republic of Texas, migrated to the Southwest hoping that the climate might improve their failing health. Ben Milam and Deaf Smith, heroes of the Alamo, came to Texas for the same reason.

Billy Mac Jones, Texas Tech history professor, has written a paper about famous people who came here to shed illness. They include O. Henry, the writer; John Nance Garner, who was to become vice-president of the U.S., and C. W. Post, the cereal king.

FORGOTTEN MAN — In 1903, Governor-elect S. W. T. Lanham and his family had to walk unescorted from their hotel to the state capitol for the inaugural ceremonies.

In the excitement of the occasion, the inaugural committee simply forgot to make any arrangements to get the new Governor to the oath-taking ceremonies.

TAXPAYERS' FRIEND — Governor James Stephen Hogg did much of his own clerical work in order to save money for the state.

In 1893, Governor Hogg — who ran the entire Executive Department with one secretary, a typist and a porter — finally was prevailed upon to request a $1,500 appropriation for a file clerk. The Legislature approved the request, but the Governor vetoed it because funds in the state treasury were low.

"I can and will add one or two more hours of service a day to the other employees of the department and do some extra work myself," the Governor said in his veto message.

STRANGE LEGACY — When Gov. James Stephen Hogg died in Houston March 3, 1906, his last wish was this: "Plant at my head a pecan tree and at my feet an old-fashioned walnut; and when these trees shall bear, let the pecans and the walnuts be given to the plain people of Texas so that they may plant them and make Texas a land of trees."

This wish was carried out, and twenty years after Hogg was buried in the State Cemetery at Austin, the first crop was harvested and 40 budded pecan trees were "given among the plain people of Texas." As time passed, however, the memorial trees began to fail. The walnut quit bearing in 1957, and the single pecan rarely bears now.

DEARLY BELOVED — Texans generally have thought well of their governors, but public esteem for that office has never been higher than it was during the term of Governor William P. Hobby.

At a wedding of two of the Mansion servants, the minister intoned: "In the presence of the Governor of Texas and Almighty God, I pronounce you man and wife."

FIRESIDE CHATS — Governor W. Lee O'Daniel was the first Texas chief executive to deliver radio talks from the Governor's Mansion to the citizens of the state.

OFFICIAL FORGER — Hugh Green, a Negro porter who served every Texas governor from O. B. Colquitt to W. Lee O'Daniel, was a self-taught expert who became adept at imitating the handwriting of his bosses.

As a result, he was frequently called upon to sign correspondence and even official state papers for the governor.

INAUGURAL NOTE — W. Lee O'Daniel was the only Governor in this century who did not take his oath of office at the Capitol. He was sworn in at Memorial Stadium on the University of Texas campus.

DINNER PARTY — When Governor W. Lee O'Daniel was inaugurated for a second term in 1941, he invited all Texans to attend his inaugural dinner.

More than 20,000 took him at his word and showed up at the Executive Mansion in Austin. The mansion grounds and even adjacent streets became an outdoor dining room. The guests ate 19,000 pounds of barbecue, 1,000 pounds of potato salad, 1,300 pounds of onions and 1,300 pickles, washing it all down with 32,000 cups of coffee sweetened with 1,000 pounds of sugar.

IT'S THE LAW — In Texas it's possible to be elected governor even if you can't qualify as a voter.

At least one successful candidate — W. Lee O'Daniel — hadn't paid his poll tax and couldn't vote for himself when he was first elected in 1938.

THE BEATNIK RANGER — Peter H. Bell, Texas Ranger, Congressman and later Governor of Texas, would have cut a fashionable figure today. He wore his hair shoulder-length and waved.

His beatnik hairdo rarely evoked comment, however. Even the bravest would-be jester respected the bowie knife and two pistols that Bell always carried in his belt.

FROM RANGER TO GOVERNOR — Peter H. Bell is the only former Texas Ranger to become Governor of Texas.

Famed for his fearlessness and marksmanship, Bell commanded a Ranger force almost until the day he was elected the third Governor of Texas.

FOUR BITS THAT MADE A GOVERNOR — Oran Milo Roberts almost missed being Governor of Texas because he didn't have 50 cents in his pocket.

Although Roberts was a successful Tyler lawyer, he didn't have a half dollar in his pocket to pay for a telegram to the State Democratic Convention telling them he would accept the gubernatorial nomination. A friend loaned him the money, Roberts sent the wire and went on to win the election of 1878.

NEVADA PICKED HIM — John Sparks, a six-foot, five-inch Lampasas County native, became the first Texan ever to govern another state when he was elected in 1903 as the chief executive of Nevada.

An ex-teamster who once freighted wagons between Lampasas, Austin and Houston, Sparks migrated to Nevada before the turn of the century. His Alamo Farms, outside of Reno, were the headquarters for a ranching empire that spread over seven million acres in Nevada, Idaho and Utah.

Entering politics, Sparks ran for the governorship as a Silver Democrat and won the office easily. After his first four-year term, he was re-elected for another term in 1907 but died a year later. He is buried in Reno.

The Wild Blue Yonder

SHY PILOT — The Midland Airport played an important role in one of the world's most publicized romances. It involved a young aviator and a diplomat's daughter.

In the late 1920's, the young pilot used to land at Midland to refuel while en route to Mexico City to see his girl. Mrs. Hall DeGarmo, wife of the airport owner, always offered him a cup of coffee.

The flyer always refused, then drove two miles down the road and bought a cup of coffee. The shy pilot, who preferred to drink his coffee alone, was Charles A. Lindbergh on his way to see Anne Morrow, daughter of the U.S. Ambassador to Mexico.

HISTORY'S HOAX—OR WAS IT? — On April 19, 1897, the Dallas *Morning News* solemnly reported that a strange airship from outer space had crashed in the Wise County town of Aurora.

For three quarters of a century, the story was regarded as a hoax. By 1973, however, the world (including some reputable scientists) were having another look.

The 1897 news story was written by an Aurora cotton merchant named E. E. Hayden and was generally regarded as a joke. Mr. Hayden, so the story goes, was so concerned when the railroad by-passed Aurora that he decided to fabricate the story of the space ship to focus attention on the town.

In the article for the Dallas *News*, he said that an airship believed to be from another planet had crashed on the farm of a prominent citizen. The pilot's body was mangled beyond recognition, but the story declared that it was clear that "he was not an inhabitant of this world."

Interestingly enough, there were other stories published in Texas and elsewhere about the same date reporting the sighting of what appeared to be an airship. On the same date, a Stephenville resident reported seeing a heavier-than-air-machine land in his pasture. He said that two men jumped out and worked on the machine.

In the spring of 1973, the site of the supposed Aurora crash finally got the attention of scientific investigators. Using electronic detectors, they reported finding many pieces of strnage metal which they have not been able to identify as anything known on earth. Within an area of 30 feet around the site where Hayden said the craft landed, the ground gives off an identical electronic response even though no metal has been found there.

Nobody knows exactly where the pilot was supposedly buried. But investigators found an isolated, unmarked grave in the Aurora cemetery which gave off the same weird electronic response that led them to the strange metal pieces.

ACES WITH BIRDSHOT — At one time during World War I, the U.S. planned to blast enemy fighter planes out of the sky with sawed-off shotguns!

In 1917, when The University of Texas began training combat airmen at its School of Aeronautics in Austin, trap shooting was a required course for the fly-boys. Adolph Topperwein, probably the best marksman with a rifle, pistol or shotgun in history, was the instructor. The future aviators, standing atop high wooden towers erected on the campus, fired pump shotguns with sawed-off barrels at clay pigeons.

The object was to teach them to hit a moving target at 75 yards. It was believed that U.S. fighter planes armed with the shotguns could down almost any enemy aircraft with which they came in contact.

HOT AIR OVER TEXAS — On April 23, 1924, the best balloon pilots in America gathered in San Antonio hoping to set a new world's record for this type of aircraft.

Kelly Field was the launch site and seven balloons were entered in the National Elimination Balloon Race. At. Stake was a $1,000 first prize, the chance to beat the existing distance record of 1,896 miles and a chance to go to Belgium to represent the U.S. in the Gordon Bennett Cup Races. Each balloon carried a pilot and co-pilot.

Three of the seven entrants failed to cover as much as 1,000 miles before their crafts came to the ground. The winner traveled 1,100 miles in 44 hours and finally landed near Rochester, Minn. But nobody came close to setting a new record, although three finalists did go on to the Belgian race. They failed to place there, too.

IT STARTED HERE — Military aviation was born in Texas.

In 1910,the Army Signal Corps sent an officer and eight men to Fort Sam Houston to establish an "aviation section." The contingent was given the Army's only plane — a pusher-type, Wright brothers bi-plane powered with a 25 horsepower water-cooled engine. The officer, Lt. Benjamin D. Foulois, had but one order: to teach himself how to fly.

He succeeded, and on March 4, 1911, he set a new world speed record by flying the 116 miles from Laredo to Eagle Pass in two hours and seven minutes.

HAVE YOU EVER WONDERED — What happened to the "Enola Gay," the B-29 that flew over Hiroshima, Japan, on August 6, 1945, and dropped the first atomic bomb in history?

Only the Air Force knows for sure what happened to the "Enola Gay" and it isn't saying. But the propeller from the historic plane is in daily service at Texas A&M University. At least, aviation experts think so.

The aluminum propeller which has operated the wind tunnel at the A&M airport since 1959 is a special design for use on planes carrying atomic bombs. Aerospace engineers are certain that it came off the "Enola Gay."

HERE FLIES THE BRIDE — One of Texas' first airborne weddings took place on January 20, 1911, when Miss Marie Shelton and W. Walter Stowe were married 1,000 feet above San Antonio's San Pedro Park.

The ceremony was read for the couple as they stood in the gondola of a balloon.

LINDY'S LUCK — The only time an airplane accident threatened the life of Charles A. Lindbergh was over Texas skies.

It was in 1925 while Lindbergh was a flying cadet at the Air Corps Advanced Flying School at Kelly Field in San Antonio. Just a week before he was to receive his wings in March of that year, Lindbergh's plane and that of another cadet collided in mid-air during a training formation.

The young man who was to become the world hero of aviation parachuted to safety.

THE CASE OF THE BATTY BOMBERS — During World War II, millions of Texas free-tailed bats faced the prospect of being drafted by the U.S. Army. They were to carry incendiary bombs into enemy territory.

Army scientists counted on the unique ability of the bats to awaken from hibernation within a few seconds. The plan was to strap a small bomb to each bat's chest, then refrigerate the animals into forced hibernation at 40° F. Planes then would drop crates of the sleeping bats over enemy cities.

Tests proved that the animals would awaken as they dropped into the warm air and would take refuge in the nearest building. There they would chew the straps off their chests and leave the bombs on their roost.

Development of the atom bomb made the incendiary project impractical, and the bats were never called to active duty.

WHO WAS THE FIRST TO FLY? — It was a Texan, not the Wright brothers, who built and flew the first airplane.

In 1865, almost 40 years before the Wright brothers got airborne at Kitty Hawk, N.C., a Fredericksburg school teacher made a powered flight before witnesses outside of San Antonio.

He was Joseph Brodbeck, who actually built and flew a heavier-than-air craft powered by a giant coil spring. His strange airplane flew for several seconds and reached tree-top height before crashing. Brodbeck never rebuilt it.

WHO WAS SECOND? — Records show that at least three Texans flew airplanes before Orville and Wilbur Wright got theirs off the ground at Kitty Hawk, N.C., in 1903.

The longest and most successful of these flights was by W. D. Custead, a railroad ticket agent in the McLennan County town of Tokio. In 1897, according to old newspaper files, Custead flew a powered plane of his own design from Tokio to Elm Mott and return, a distance of five miles.

Custead's partner was Gustave Whitehead of Bridgeport, Conn., and the two continued to improve their model. On August 18, 1901, Custead flew the plane — which had 80-inch wings that actually flapped — for a half mile at the Bridgeport airport.

The plane was such a success that Texas financiers raised money to put it into production, but nothing ever came of it.

RIDE 'EM COWBOY — A cowboy and a mechanic became the nation's temporary air heroes by setting an endurance record in the Texas skies.

On Sunday, May 19, 1929, Reg Robbins and James Kelly, the mechanic and the cowboy, climbed into a rebuilt Ryan monoplane at Fort Worth's Meacham Field and took off. When they landed seven days later, they had been aloft for 172 1/2 hours to set a new record for continuous flight.

For their feat, the pair received two new airplanes and $50,000 in cash — about 50 times the military pay received by today's astronauts for their forays into outer space.

FEET ON THE GROUND — Airville, in northeastern Bell County, is air-minded in name only. It has no airport and there isn't a qualified pilot in town.

TIP-OFF ON TIPPLERS — The School of Aerospace Medicine at Brooks Air Force Base, San Antonio, has developed a gas chromatograph which, by measuring chemicals in the atmosphere, may be able to sniff out possible signs of life on other planets.

Don't be surprised, however, if police departments adopt the device first. It is such a supersensitive sniffer that it can detect alcohol in a man's saliva from a bottle of beer he drank the day before!

THE BIBLE AIRLINE — An Old Testament prophet helped to give Texas its first airline two years before the Wright brothers proved that man could fly.

A Bible-reading Texan became intrigued with the first chapter of Ezekiel wherein the writer recounts a parable in which men equipped with four wings and wheels flew like birds. From this and other Biblical accounts, a plan to build an airplane grew.

Ezekiel Airship Manufacturing Co. of Pittsburg, Tex., actually got a charter in 1901 and an airplane was built. The plane did make a series of hedgehop flights around East Texas (about as far and as high as the Wright brothers did later at Kitty Hawk). However, the Texas financial backers pulled out and it became necessary to find new capital.

The plane was loaded on a flatcar to be taken to Chicago for a demonstration before potential investors. At Texarkana, however, a tornado struck the train, blew the plane to the ground and destroyed it. That ended the experiment.

Lawmen

LEGENDS THAT LIE — Every Texan older than age five knows the story of the riot-torn oil boom town in the early 1930's that sent out a call for the Rangers to restore order.

Local gendarmes formed a welcoming committee at the railroad station and could only blink in disbelief when a single Texas Ranger got off the train.

"You mean the Governor sent only one Ranger?" somebody asked.

"Well, you've only got one riot, haven't you?" was the laconic reply.

It is one of the most often told tales of Texas, but no historian has ever been able to prove that it happened.

Both Dr. Walter Prescott Webb, the unofficial Ranger historian, and the late Col. Homer Garrison, Jr., head of the Department of Public Safety from 1935 to 1968, spent years trying to authenticate the story. Neither ever succeeded.

THE GOOD OLD DAYS? — Frank A. Hamer, Jr., who spent 50 years as a city marshal, Texas Ranger and private investigator, never denied the legend which said that he had killed 53 men.

He survived 49 known gunfights, was left for dead seven times by outlaws, had 23 scars from gunshot wounds and still carried 16 bullets in his body when he died peacefully in his sleep in 1955 at the age of 71.

BIRTH OF THE FIVE-GUN — Samuel Colt invented the revolver in Connecticut, but the Texas Rangers proved its effectiveness.

The U.S. Army disdained Colt's five-shot revolver as useless, but Texas ordered 227 of the guns for its Rangers. And in June, 1844, when Comanches attacked Captain Jack Hays and his Rangers along the Pedernales River northwest of San Antonio, the revolver proved its superiority.

When the 100 Indians attacked, Hays and his men fired their rifles first. The Indians, expecting the Rangers to dismount and reload, regrouped for a second attack. Instead, the Rangers charged, firing a steady and withering fusillade at 15 to 20 paces. Almost every Comanche in the raiding party died.

From then on, the Colt revolver was an imperishable part of the West.

IT TAKES ALL KINDS — Many a Negro and Mexican-American has proudly worn the badge of a Texas Ranger.

Since the Rangers were created in 1835 as three companies of "mounted riflemen" to protect the borders and enforce the laws of the new Republic of Texas, their roster has included men of almost every race and creed. At one time, there was a Ranger company made up almost entirely of Negroes.

Even Yellow Wolf, a Quahadi Comanche, wore the famed star-in-a-circle badge. He was one of Captain Peter F. Ross's Rangers.

RANGE OF THE RANGERS — The Texas Rangers are one of the few law enforcement agencies that can go anywhere in the world to get their man.

Not only are they charged with keeping the peace over more than 250,000 square miles and 13 million population that is Texas, but the half hundred members of the Ranger force can, and do, roam the world. When they find a Texas law-breaker, however, they must have him arrested by local authorities.

THE ORIGINAL LONE RANGER — Unlike his television counterpart, the original "Lone Ranger" never wore a mask and he almost always traveled alone.

He was John R. Hughes, a poetry-writing, Bible-reading tenderfoot who came to Texas from Illinois in 1885 to find solitude as a rancher. He became a lawman instead and soon was the most feared Ranger west of the Pecos.

Outlaws swore that he knew every curve of the Rio Grande from its mouth to El Paso, a 1,200-mile stretch that he often traveled alone. They claimed that he knew criminals so well that often he could name the culprit simply by learning the circumstances surrounding the crime.

Zane Grey preserved the Hughes legend for posterity — and television — in his novel, *The Lone Star Ranger*.

GRAVEYARD PHILOSOPHY — The stone over the grave where Texas Ranger Captain Bill McDonald is buried near Quanah, Hardeman County, carries this legend:

"No man that's in the wrong can stand up against a fellow that's in the right and keep a-comin'."

HOLD-UP MAN — Ben Thompson, famed city marshal of Austin in the 1880's, held up more trains than Jesse James ever did — but for a different purpose.

Ben's greatest pleasure was in stopping his buggy across the tracks in front of an express train at the Austin depot, covering the engineer with his gun and forcing him to hold the train while Thompson called an acquaintance from the platform and talked with him.

When the marshal had finished his conversation — which sometimes lasted as long as half an hour — he would holster his gun, drive his buggy off the tracks and signal the engineer to go ahead.

SECRET RANGER — When Woodrow Wilson was campaigning for the presidency in 1912, a Texas Ranger was his constant bodyguard.

Wilson's opponent was President William Howard Taft, and the campaign was long and bitter. When several threats were made against Wilson's life, his closest advisor, Colonel E. M. House of Austin, sent for the Rangers.

House selected Captain Bill McDonald, one of the most colorful members of the Ranger force. That ended the threats on the life of the future president.

RANGER'S TOWN — Oakland, Calif., is the only city in the country that can claim an ex-Texas Ranger as its founder.

He was Colonel Jack Hays, who migrated to California after many years as a Ranger and Indian fighter in Texas. In 1850, he was elected sheriff of San Francisco County. On March 3, 1852, he joined with five friends to purchase the land that was to become the townsite of Oakland. Shortly after the purchase, he moved his home to the area and became one of the new town's first settlers.

INDEX

Abilene, city of, 119
Acton State Park, smallest in U.S., 116
Adobe Walls, Battle of, 17
Adolphus Hotel, Dallas, 63
Airville, village of, 140
Alamo, The:
  forgotten by Texas, 17
  only 32 volunteers, 43
  hoax of Crockett's memoirs, 78
  second commander, 79
  McArdle's painting of, 81
  Moses Rose, coward of, 102-103
  Bowie and Milam, heroes of, 124
Alabama-Coushatta Indians, 80, 101
Albany, town of, 118
Albion's Ferry, 109
Algoa, town of, 58
Alibates Ranch and flint quarry, 91
Allen, Maj. Terry, 63
Alley Oop, origin of comic strip, 74
Alpine, city of, on the Chihuahua Trail, 65, 102
Alto, town of, 122
Altoga, town of, 59
Amarillo, city of, 91, 110
Amichel, first name for Texas, 106
Anahuac, town of, 104
Anaqua, town of, 54
Andrew Female College, 29
Anderson County, 59
Arlen, Richard, motion picture star, 52
Arnold, Maj. Ripley A., 46
Armstrong, A. Joseph, 120
Aspermont, town of, 109
Associated Press, The, 14
Audubon, John James, naturalist in Texas, 24
Aurora, town of, 136
Austin County, 40
Austin, city of:
  Gen. Custer resident of, 23
  barbed wire developed in, 39, 63, 64, 74, 80, 81
  one of seven capitals of Texas, 102
  home of the Carlotta mirrors, 104, 127
  murder at the Capitol, 128, 135, 143
Austin, Stephen F., 23
Automobile, first in Texas, 93

B

Bache, Richard, only vote against statehood, 40
Bailey, Britton, wanted to be buried standing up, 23-24

Bailey, Mollie, circus owner, 27
Bailey's Prairie, 24
Barbed Wire:
  developed in Austin, 39
  sold by J. W. Gates, 86
Barrett, Lynis T., first oil man, 35
Barrera, Manuel, made first coins, 96
Barrymore, Maurice, once shot in Marshall, 97
Bartlett & Western Railway, "Route of the Apostles," 87
Barziza, Decimus et Ultimus, 89
Bass, Sam, failure as outlaw, 99
Bastrop County, 60, 77
Bathing Suit, first "topless", 28
Bathtub, world's largest, 114
Battle of Flowers Parade, origin of, 106

Baugh, Capt. John J., 79
Baylor County, 101, 118
Baylor, Judge R. E. B., 25
Baylor University:
  first coeducational school, 29
  most lucrative football game, 106
  Browning collection, 120

Beaumont, city of, 21
Bean, Judge Roy:
  how town of Langtry named, 51
  as boxing promoter, 78
Bee County, famous hanging in, 84
Beeville, city of, 84
Belton, city of, home of Sanctificationist Sisters, 30
Bell County, 140
Bell, Gov. Peter H., 134
Benton, Jesse James, composer of "Oh, Bury Me Not," 63
Best, town of, how named, 58
Bexar County, 51
Big Bend:
  wild Longhorns, 62
  "Texas-size" asparagus, 71
Big Lake, oil boom, 58
Big Spring, Neb., 99
Big Thicket:
  ghost light of, 71
  facts about, 118-119
Blessing, town of, 54
Boerne, city of, 24
Boggess, I. H., founder of St. Jo, 40
Booker, town of, town that migrated, 57
Booth, John Wilkes, maybe died in Texas, 20
Bonham, city of:
  location of Rayburn Library, 57
  on Chihuahua Trail, 65

145

Bonham, James Butler, original
beatnik, 103
Borden, A. P., developer of Brahma
cattle, 65
Borden, Gail, editor of *Texas Telegraph
and Register*, 94
Bow, Clara, starred in "Wings" made at
San Antonio, 52
Bowie, James:
as a con man, 95
in first land speculations, 124-125
Brackettville, town of, 18
Brands, Cattle, new methods of, 63
Brazoria County, 24
Brazos County, 120
Brazos River, 38, 53, 120
Brazzil, Ruth Virginia, special Supreme
Court justice, 29
Brodbeck, Joseph, first man to fly, 139
Brooks Air Force Base, School of
Aerospace Medicine, 140
Brotherhood of Carpenters and Joiners,
one of oldest unions, 90
Brown, Frank W., researcher on early
coinage, 95
Browning, Elizabeth Barrett, library at
Baylor University, 120
Browning Library, 120
Browning, Robert, library at Baylor
University, 120
Brownsville, city of:
Civil War ended nearby, 105
buried treasure near, 111-112
Bryan, John Neely, founder of Dallas,
47
Buffalo Bayou, 18, 57
Buffalo Soldiers, name given Negro
troops, 101
Buffalo Wallow, Battle of, 18
Bug Tussle, town of, how named, 58
Burdette, Pink, composer of "Oh, Bury
Me Not," 63
Burkett, J. H., developed Burkett pecan,
9
Burleson County, 120
Burnet, David G., 38
elected president of Republic as com-
promise, 124
his hatred of Sam Houston, 129
Burnet, J. H., founder of Pasadena, 120
Butterfield Trail, 118

C

Caddo Lake:
community of Uncertain at, 48
pearls found there, 111
Calhoun County, 58

Caldwell County, 51
Camels in Texas, 37
Camp Hill Oil Field, 34
Camp Verde, 37
Canadian, town of, 17
Canadian River, 91
Canton, town of, 116
Canyon, city of, 64
Capital, First, 37
Capitals, Other, 102
Capitol Hotel, Houston, 131
Capitol, State of:

"The Cowboy" sculpture at, 64
Texas may not have title to land, 77
murder at, 79
McArdle paintings in, 81
built from a single mountain, 90
robbery in, 128

Carlsbad Caverns, 118
Casa Tijernia Pharmacy, faith cures for
sale, 91
Cash, town of, how named, 59
Cason, Charles, 64
Castroville, town of, 55
Cavity Lake, 32
Central National Road, 121
Cemetery, State:
most imposing monument in, 132
Gov. Hogg's grave, 133
Chambers, Gen. Thomas J., 77
Chaps, origin of, 67
Cheerleader Supply Co., 93
Cherokee County, 122
Cherokee Indians, 75
Chewing Gum:
first made from sap in Texas, 71-72
Santa Anna's role in development of,
72
Chihuahua Trail, 64
Childress, George C., 19
Chili:
brought to Texas, 86
live wolves helped to sell, 91-92
Christmas, first recorded celebration in
Texas, 99
Cincinnati, town of, 70
Circle Dot Ranch, 62
Circus, Mollie Bailey's, 27
Cisco, city of, 119
Civil War in Texas:
experiment with camels, 37
memorial to Union soldiers at Com-
fort, 52
how it resulted in Texas giving away
resources, 94-95
it ended on Texas soil, 105-106
Clarke, Justin (Nig), 84
Clarksville, town of, 73, 76, 109

Declaration of Independence:
not signed on March 2, 19
Mexican signers of, 76
"lost" for many years, 77
all but one original copy lost, 102-103
DeGarmo, Mrs. Hall, 136
Denison, city of: 23, 26
birthplace of ice cream soda, 39, 42, 49
has monument erected to saloonkeeper, 54, 55
birthplace of President Eisenhower, 57
has first free graded school, 58, 83
site of "war" with Oklahoma over toll bridge, 104, 115, 121
Denison *Daily News*, 84
Denison *Herald*, 14
Denton *Record-Chronicle*, 14
Dew, town of, how named, 55
D'Hanis, town of, 55
Dill, Mrs. Jack, 28
Dime Box, town of, 126
Dinosaur "capital", 50, 76
Distance across Texas, 100
Doans Crossing, of the Red River, 63
Dobie, J. Frank, 15, 71
Dodson, Mrs. Sarah Bradley, 27
Dodge City, Kans., 62
Drama, first in Texas, 19, 57
Driscoll, Clara, 17
Driskill Hotel, Austin, 104
Dublin, city of, 51, 119
Duff, Col. James, 52
Dunne, Key, 63

E

Eagle Pass, city of, has store that outfitted an army, 91, 138
Edwards County, 52
Eisenhower, President Dwight D., 57
El Paso:
city of, 19, 95
has lost gold mine, 110, 121, 142
Elliott, Keith, 22
Ellis County, 50, 52
Ellis, Richard, 19
Elm Mott, town of, 139
Elsinore Cattle Company, 62
Emancipation Day, 98
Enola Gay, The, 138
Erath County, 51, 119
Ernst, Friedrich, 40, 48
Estevan the Moor, 102
Euper, J. A., inventor of ice cream soda, 39
Excelsior House Hotel, Jefferson, 41, 48, 114

Eyes of Texas, The, 103
Ezekiel Airship Manufacturing Co., 140

F

Fair, State of Texas, 105
Fairy, town of, how named, 59
Falcon Dam, on Rio Grande River, 50
Fallersblen, Hoffman von, 22
Falls County, 60, 99
Fannin County, 58
Farr, Joe, 199
Fayette County, 116, 128
Fenley, Guy, 33
Ferguson, Gov. James E., 129
Ferguson, Gov. Miriam A., 126, 129
Finck, H. W., 88
Fink, town of, 49
Finger Furniture Store, in Houston, 90
Sammy Finger, 90
"First Monday", how Canton's began, 116
First National Bank of Lubbock, 115
Fitzsimmons, Bob, 79
Flag, Lone Star:
designer of the first, 27
locomotives must display, 83
Flags, Other, seven, not six, flags over Texas, 106-107
Flying Saucer, first sighted in U.S., 84
Ford, Col. John S. (Rip):
how he helped prolong Civil War, 41
how last shot of Civil War fired under his command, 105
Forests:
35 million acres of, 100
largest stand of miniature Harvard oaks in U.S., 122
Fort Concho, 46
Fort Davis, 73
as home of "Buffalo Soldiers," 102
Fort Clark, most Army brass served there, 18, 52
Fort Griffin, 118
Fort Griffin "Fandangle", 118
Fort Quitman, 116
Fort Sam Houston:

movie, "Wings," produced there, 52
birthplace of military aviation, 138
Fort Stockton, town of, 65
Fort Worth, city of:

originated Texas' first television program, 22, 39
origin of slogan, "Where the West begins," 46, 76
home of first bank headed by a Negro, 87, 122, 139

Foulois, Benjamin D., father of military aviation, 138
Frame, Myrtle, 52
Francke, Louis, 128
Fraternal Bank & Trust Co. of Fort Worth, 87
Fredericksburg, city of, 25th anniversary of founding, 25, 98, 114
Freestone County, 55
French Embassy, 81
Friendswood, town of, 88
Fruits, of Texas, 100
Fuchs, Adolph, 22
Funerals, laws governing them in Texas, 82

G

Gaines County, 89
Galveston, city of:
  John J. Audubon painted there, 24, 38
  sent only delegate that voted against statehood, 40
  build first golf course, 53
  first city to levy school tax, 58, 70
  financed first public hospital, 81
  home of unusual labor union, 89, 97, 121
  headquarters of pirate Jean Lafitte, 132
Galveston County, 58, 88
Galveston Island, 95, 102
Garner, Vice President John Nance, 133
Garza County, 24
Garza, Joe Antonio de la, 94
Gates, John W. (Bet-a-Million), 86
German Settlers:
  songs about, 22
  Friedrich Ernst, 40
  first town built by, 48
  settlement named for flag, 50
  brought chili to Texas, 86
  made peace with Indians, 98
  last remaining Wend settlers, 121
Georgetown, city of, 107
Gebhardt, William, 86
Gilchrist, Gibb, 116
Gillespie County, 52
Gladewater, city of, 33
Glass Mountains, 62
Glen Rose:
  town of, 20
  unofficial "dinosaur capital," 50, 76
Glidden, Joseph F., 39
Godos, Don Miguel Farfan de los, 20
God's Little Acreage, 45
God's Mercy Store, 121
Gold in Texas, 87, 122
Golf Course, first in Texas, 53

Gonzales, city of, 43
Goodbread, Joseph G., 105
Goodnight, Charles, 66
Gordon, F. J., 20
Goucher, Samuel, 77
Gould, Jay, 41
Governor, First, 125
Governor's Mansion:
  Napoleon's clock in, 74
  had no bathroom for years, 124
  Governor pays for entertainment in, 126
  only one guest room in, 127
  lack of heat in, 130
  Legislature pays for upkeep, 132
Governor's Office, Facts about:
  Cost of maintaining, 75
  new locks for each occupant, 125
  only one occupant died in office, 127
  heaviest occupant, 129
  one occupant rode mule, 132
  one occupant did own clerical work, 133
  first occupant to deliver radio talks, 134
  one occupant sworn in at football stadium, 134
Goyens, William, 120
Granbury, town of, 20
Granger, Gen. Gordon, 97
Granite Mountain, 90
Grant, Gen. U. S.:
  at Fort Clark, 18
  at Corpus Christi, 75
  at Jefferson, 114
Grayson, Peter W., 127
Green, Col. E. H. R., 87, 93
Green, Mrs. Hetty, 87
Green, Hugh, 134
Greer County, 84
Gregg, Josiah, 28
Grey, Zane, 142
Gringo, origin of term, 69
Grinninger, John, 39
Groce's Ferry, 38
Guadalupe River, 60
Gulf of Mexico, 24, 65, 102

H

Hamer, Frank A., Jr., 141
Hamilton County, 59
Hamilton, James, 43
Hamlin, V. T., 74
Hanging, Last Public, 84
Hardeman County, 143
Hardin County, 32, 71
Harlin, Harry W., 48

Harrisburg, town of, 102
Harrison County:
  community of Uncertain, 48
  how county seat was selected, 52, 58,
  111
Harrison, President Benjamin, 106
Hart, Weldon, 51, 127
Hartley County, 117
Harvey House Restaurant, in Marshall,
  Harrison County, 97
Hat, Ten Gallon, 64
Hayden, E. E., 136
Hays, Jack, 142, 143
Heidingsfelder, Charles E., Jr., 56
Hemphill County, 17
Henderson, city of, 87
Henenberg, Hattie L., 29
Henry, O., 133
Hereford Cattle, 62
Herkimer, Lawrence R., 93
Herm, R. C., 48
Hermleigh, town of, 48
Hidalgo County, 94, 113
Hobby, Sr., Gov. W. P., 130, 133
Hogg, Miss Ima, 28, 74
Hogg, Gov. James Stephen, 28
  his veto of appropriation to purchase
  San Jacinto Battleground, 44
  first governor to deliver speech by
  phonograph, 105, 128
Hogg, Tom, 28
Hood County, 20, 116
House, Col. Edward M., 125, 143
Houston, Andrew Jackson, 128
Houston Bank & Trust Co., 89
Houston Baseball Museum, 90
Houston, city of:
  burial place of only Federal woman
  soldier, 27
  as oil center, 35, 44, 56
  first professional theater, 57
  population increase, 59, 64
  as producer of honey, 75, 89, 90
  as capital of Texas, 102
  description of city flag, 115, 121, 131,
  135
Houston County, 122
Houston, Sam:
  mentioned in anecdotes, 24, 25
  use of steamboat *Yellowstone*, 38
  incident at theater performance, 57
  his efforts to ban banks, 92-93, 98
  his halting of Regulator-Moderator
  War, 105, 110, 126
  his dislike by David G. Burnet, 129
  his failure to accept Samuel F. B.
  Morse invention, 130
  his "indecent" portrait, 131
  politician's dream, 131

Houston Ship Channel, 18
Houston Stock Exchange, 56
Houston & Texas Central Railway, 39
Houston, University of, 106
Howell, Joe, 40
Hubbard, Richard B., 129
Hudspeth County, 116
Hughes, Capt. John R., 142
Huisar, Peter, 69
Hunt County, 59
Huntsville, city of, 83
Huston, Tom, 87
Hyer, Dr. Robert S., 107

I

Ice Cream Soda, invented in Texas, 39
Indians, Most, 49
Industry, town of, 41, 48
Institute of Texan Cultures, 71, 74, 75
International Business Machines Corp.,
  100
International Longshoremen's Associa-
  tion, 89
Iraan, town of, 74

J

Jackrabbit, 70
Jackson, Charles W., 105
J and J Club, 119
Jefferson, town of, 41, 58, 111, 114
Jesus Christ, 121
Jessie Allen Wise Garden Club, 114
Jester, Gov. Beauford H., 127
Jim Turner, The, 109
Joe Roughneck Park, 33
Johnson County, 59
Johnson Parks, 83
Johnson, President Lyndon B., 80, 107,
  131
Johnston, J. E., 23
Jones, President Anson:
  costly note, 92
  died a suicide, 131-132
  came to Texas for health, 132
Jones, Billy Mac, 133
Jones, Enoch, 51
Jones, John Rice, 93
Julian Bivins Museum, 28
Junction City, Kans., 68

K

Kansas City Southern Railway, 45
Kaufman County, 64
Katy Railroad, 21
Keeler, W. W. (Bill), 75